THE KEY TO SU

Lie in the dark and listen,
It's clear tonight so they're flying high,
Hundreds of them, thousands perhaps
Riding the icy, moonlight sky.
Men, machinery, bombs and maps,
Altimeters and guns and charts,
Coffee, sandwiches, fleece-lined boots,
Bones and muscles and minds and hearts,
English saplings with English roots
Deep in the earth they've left below.
Lie in the dark and let them go,
Lie in the dark and listen.

Lie in the dark and listen,
They're going over in waves and waves,
High above villages, hills and streams.
Country churches and little graves
And little citizens' worried dreams.
Very soon they'll have reached the sea
And far below them will lie the bays
And cliffs and sands where they used to be
Taken for summer holidays.
Lie in the dark and let them go,
Theirs is a world we'll never know.
Lie in the dark and listen.

Lie in the dark and listen.
City magnates and steel contractors,
Factory workers and politicians,
Soft hysterical little actors,
Ballet dancers, reserved musicians,
Safe in your warm civilian beds
Count your profits and count your sheep
Life is passing over your heads.

Just turn over and try to sleep.
Lie in the dark and let them go,
There's one debt you'll forever owe:
Lie in the dark and listen.

Nöel Coward

Kenneth A. Harder DFC, FRSA

The Key to Survival
Bomber Command in World War II

Foreword by Air Marshal Sir Ivor Broom
KCB, CBE, DSO, DFC**, AFC

GEORGE MANN *of* MAIDSTONE

THE KEY TO SURVIVAL
by Kenneth A. Harder DFC, FRSA

First published by George Mann 2006

ISBN 0 7041 0414 8

Kenneth A. Harder DFC, FRSA
has asserted his right under Section 77 of the
Copyright, Designs and Patents Act 1998
to be identified as the author of this book

Printed and bound in Great Britain by
Woolnough Bookbinders Ltd
Irthlingborough, Northampton
for George Mann Books, PO Box 22
Maidstone, in the English County of Kent

I dedicate this book
with all my love
to my late wife

To Ken
with best wishes

Ken Harden

635 Path finder Squad.

Contents

Illustrations

Author's Introduction

In this book I have aimed to outline the history of air warfare, particularly the strategy and development of weaponry in relation to the Royal Air Force and the 8th USAAF up to and including WW2. It is hoped it will help the student and encourage the general reader to increase their knowledge of the impact made by the air arm on military conflict and an enemy's economy, especially where operations against major German cities were involved. I have also tried to answer some of the critics who, even today, state that both Bomber Command and Arthur Harris did little to aid the war effort and were guilty of both terrorism and war crimes.

Those who served in Bomber Command, like their comrades in the Merchant Navy, received no official recognition for their wartime service. Yet without their effort it is possible that Hitler's scientists would have completed their development of V3 and V4 rockets, the advanced jet fighter and possibly finalised their work on an atomic bomb. At the very least this could have led to more years of war, at the worst it could have cost us our freedom.

My research has involved reading many books, and magazine and newspaper articles from which I have quoted liberally in the hope that readers will study them and find the true balance between those who justify and those who condemn. At the end of the day we have to remember the sacrifice of the crews who set out in their thin metal planes flying their missions by night and day against the might of the opposing forces in the belief that their efforts would shorten the war. All quotations have been listed with the publications, authors and publishers duly acknowledged.

An additional list of books by authors, some of whom played an active role in the air war, has been included which should assist understanding the events which took place.

Foreword

by

Air Marshal Sir Ivor Broom KCB, CBE, DSO, DFC**, AFC.

The role of RAF Bomber Command in World War II and the contribution which it made to the overall war effort is extensively reviewed in this book. The author points out that bombing was neither very accurate nor effective in the first three years of the war — primarily through lack of navigational and bombing aids. But this all changed in 1942/3 with new navigation/bombing aids, the introduction of four engined bombers, and the formation of the Pathfinder Force to mark the targets for the main force bombers.

The author quotes the views of some two hundred other writers of books about World War II — many of them distinguished historians. Some writers supported the bomber offensive, others criticised it — but nowhere do any of the critics, even with hindsight, produce an alternative strategy for the years when we stood alone. A sound defence, by itself, will never win a war and the book shows how a great part of the German Industrial Effort was progressively devoted towards fending off the bomber attacks to the detriment of the development of their attack forces. German and Allied Generals also all comment on the effectiveness of the bombing in support of Allied Ground Forces as those forces progressively moved across Europe to final victory.

This is a very balanced book and would form a good basis for teaching the present generation the history of the Bomber Offensive in World War II — an Offensive which Hitler's Armament Minister Albert Speer described as "the greatest lost battle for Germany".

Preface

For centuries Man had long wished to emulate the birds and fly. History records that Icarus and Leonardo da Vinci studied and experimented with designs to attain that goal without success. Eventually it was two Frenchmen who first overcame gravity by rising from the earth in a balloon on 5 June 1783. Like most discoveries it was soon to be used for military purposes, first by the French in 1794. Other nationals, including those of America and Britain, experimented with ballooning in the 19th century and also used them for military operations. It is however the 20th century that can truly be termed the 'air age', for that is when Mankind truly learned to fly.

In its infancy, at the beginning of the twentieth century, the first heavier than air flight took place, the dreams of Icarus and da Vinci were finally realised and it came of age in the 1940's . . . and so the quest for air supremacy began.

Chapter One

'To be prepared for war is one of the effectual means of preserving peace.'

George Washington - 1790

THE DISCOVERY OF HOW TO FLY HAS CHANGED THE whole concept of waging war. It has become mobile and every citizen of warring countries is now a combatant.

No longer do armies have to face each other with musket and cannon, or dig trenches and shell each other, each side trying to break the deadlock by brief forays across no-man's-land in endless endeavours to take a few pitiful yards, leaving hundreds' sometimes thousands' of dead and wounded upon the battlefield. In modern warfare the phrase, 'A nation at war', means just that, the whole nation's economy and all of its people are involved. It is total war.

Orville and Wilbur Wright were brothers, the first men to fly a heavier than air machine in December 1903. Louis Bleriot flew the English Channel in 1909. It then took only two years for the aeroplane to be adapted as a weapon of war for aerial bombing in Italy's annexation of Libya.

The writing was plain on the wall. Leading world powers began to consider air armament. But most of their military leaders had little time for this new-fangled weapon. Indeed at the commencement of World War I the aeroplane was only considered useful for the observation of the movement of ground forces and for ranging artillery. Whilst the Navy initially considered it being of use as a platform for a gun, they did later in the war conduct, 'successful strategic bombing against Zeppelin sheds in Germany and enemy bases in Belgium, besides sinking warships by torpedo'. [1]

In time the tactical advantage of bombing enemy supply lines was appreciated. By 1915 it became clear that the enemy must be prevented from observations over our lines and the need for fighter planes was recognised. In due course they arrived at the battlefronts. Later the possibilities of attacking enemy transport centres and industries led to the commencement of strategic air warfare and the introduction of the strategic bomber.

But, as so often happens, there was a lack of interest by the military. It was individual inventors who developed the bombsight and the machine gun which could fire through the propeller. The Germans used Zeppelins and Gotha aircraft to bomb English Coastal towns, the Midlands, Scotland and London, which latter raids caused widespread public outrage at the lack of air defence. But still the contribution that the aeroplane could make to the Allied war effort was largely ignored.

On July 11th 1917 at a War Cabinet meeting it was agreed that Prime Minister Lloyd George and General Jan Smuts (later Field Marshal) should examine the 'air organisation and the direction of aerial operations'. It was the best committee possible, two elected members with one usually absent. Within a few weeks, on 17th August, Smuts produced a remarkable document. It recommended that an Air Ministry should be formed together with a separate fighting service in which the Royal Flying Corps and the Royal Naval Air Service should be absorbed.

Then with amazing prescience he prophesied, 'the day may not be far off, when aerial operations with their devastation of enemy lands and destruction of industrial and populous centres on a vast scale may become the principal operations of war to which the older military and naval operations may become secondary and subordinate'.

So Britain became the first country to have an Air Arm

independent of the other Services. On 1st April 1918 the Royal Air Force was formed. Strategic bombing operations were small in size and, primarily, both Britain and Germany had to devote most of the Service budget to air defence rather than attack. After the Armistice the struggle for survival of Britain's new independent Air Force was intense.

There is a dispute over the actual strength of the RAF on 11th November 1918. Sir Maurice Dean (a top Air Ministry civil servant) states, 'it was speedily run down from . . . 280 Squadrons to a force one tenth of that size, mostly abroad'. [2] However, Robert Jackson states, 'on 11th November 1918, the total strength of the Royal Air Force stood at over 380 squadrons and 22,000 aircraft of all types. It was the most formidable array of air power in the world; a mighty organisation built almost from nothing in the space of four years, a force which — honed to a razor-edge in combat — had emerged from the war with an unparalleled reputation for skill and bravery that was to form the basis of a lasting tradition'. [3]

Most of these remarks could be applied with equal force to the RAF at the close of World War II.

What is beyond dispute is that within a few weeks of the end of the First World War the run down of the Royal Air Force's strength both in front line and reserves had begun. The attitude of the government of the day was indifferent as it had so many other matters with which to contend and both the Army and the Navy were hostile to the continued existence of the new Service as they wanted the return of their wartime Air Arms. These attitudes continued to exist for many years, and the search for economies in Government spending powered by the Geddes Committee in 1921 and the Colwyn Committee of 1925 continually threw up the suggestion that the Royal Air Force should be disbanded. Fortunately both Committees ignored the advice.

It should be remembered that the theory and practise of

Air Power was still in its infancy and what it could or could not do was the subject of much inadequately informed debate. The outstanding advocates of Air Power in those early years were Trenchard, Douhet and Mitchell. Hugh Trenchard, Chief of the Air Staff, saw it as a winning weapon and made great claims for the role of the Royal Air Force. Whilst the Army policy was to defeat the enemy's land forces, he said, 'the Air Force's was to defeat the enemy nation'. But he was unclear as to whether the primary aim of strategic bombing would be the destruction of the sources of military strength, factories, power supplies, lines of communication and so on, or to break the will of the enemy population to support the struggle; or a combination of the two.

In 1928 he wrote in a memorandum to the Chiefs of Staff Sub-Committee, 'Whatever we may wish or hope, and whatever course of action we may decide, whatever be the views held as to the legality, or the humanity, or the military wisdom and expediency of such operations, there is not the slightest doubt that in the next war both sides will send their aircraft out without scruple to bomb those objectives which they consider the most suitable.' [4]

The Italian General Guilo Douhet said, 'victory in the future will go to the country which can achieve air supremacy and bring the enemy to his knees by bombarding his cities'. Finally there was the United States Army Brigadier General 'Billy' Mitchell, who sought an independent rôle for the US Army Air Force. He tried demonstrating his theories by bombing old warships and challenged the Navy's claim to be the first line of national defence. He was court martialled in 1925 and resigned in 1926.

These then were the views of the early pioneers of air warfare and it can be seen that there was general agreement about the necessity for an air arm to be independent of military and naval control. They also realised that the aeroplane would inevitably change the face of warfare; so that control of the air space above and beyond where troops and ships were operating was absolutely imperative if the operations of those sister services were to succeed.

Unfortunately, the Navy would not or could not accept the idea that battleships could be sunk by bombs and the Army thought of the aeroplane in terms of the transportation of troops, equipment and supplies or as a means of support for troops in battle. So these Services continued the old squabbles and competed strongly with the Royal Air Force for more funds in the annual round of Service Estimates. And they were assisted in this by some short-sighted, irresponsible politicians of the day.

Neither the Army nor the Navy believed in the aeroplane as an offensive weapon. At the same time the national economy was under considerable strain. In the ensuing debates it became clear that unless the Air Force could shoulder some of the other Services' tasks throughout the Empire, there would be insufficient funds to continue its independence. As was to be expected, both the Army and the Navy chiefs rejected the very idea of this upstart young Service assuming any part, however small, of their traditional roles. But the Air Force believed it could not only perform with greater efficiency, but with a considerable saving to the Defence Budget, particularly where the role of the Army was concerned.

After the Great War, Britain was given the mandates of Palestine, Iraq and the Transjordan. In 1920, when rebellion broke out in these territories, the Government was faced with demands to pull out its military forces. At a conference in Cairo in 1921 Trenchard put forward the idea that the RAF could take over the Army's task of policing Iraqi territory, it being pointed out that aircraft could cover an area of ground in one day that would take the Army weeks to police. Furthermore an aircraft could catch rebels out in the open before they had time to go to ground. It was finally agreed

17

that squadrons of the RAF were to test out the idea in Iraq and the Transjordan, the result being such a resounding success that in 1922 the RAF took full responsibility for the internal security of these two territories.

The success of air control led to it being used in the Aden protectorate and on the North West Frontier in India. Thus a useful role was found and also valuable experience obtained in reconnaissance, tactical bombing and Army co-operation. If the natives got restive and rebellious, leaflets were dropped warning the villagers that a continuance of their behaviour would result in a bombing raid. If this warning was ignored another visit was made stating that their village would be attacked in the next few days. The inhabitants took off into the countryside with their goods and chattels and their hutments were bombed. Afterwards the population came back uninjured to a village they had to rebuild. The RAF got practice, the rebels were taught a lesson.

Back in the UK however, the RAF's operational strength was totally lacking in offensive capacity. In the Air Council there were differing opinions as to whether day and night bombing operations could be carried out by the same aircraft. 'The main argument favouring the developing of a bomber for night operations was that such a machine would need less armour plating and defensive firepower . . . the result a substantial reduction in weight, which meant a bigger bombload could be carried'. [5] Political ineptness, the usual tight-fistedness of the Treasury together with Mandarins in other Whitehall departments ensured that the Air Force was way below the strength that had been envisaged.

Sir Maurice Dean wrote, 'Failure to invest at a reasonable rate over the period 1922-31 was a source of real weakness when expansion finally began, after yet more delays, in 1934. Over this decade Britain was the leader and the centre of a great Empire and with great responsibilities for its defence. Britain tried to run its Empire on the cheap'. [6]

It paid for it with the loss of territories, of lives and prestige when war came. Hindsight is a wonderful thing, but the short-sighted political thinking of the time in the face of all-to-evident global unrest and the unpreparedness of our own armed forces to deal with any major conflict that might arise really beggars belief. Granted the worldwide economic depression of the late 'twenties and early 'thirties did call for the best use of available resources but the events taking place in Europe should have set the alarm bells ringing.

In Abyssinia and Somalia the use of aircraft and poison gas by the Italians against populations armed only with spears, gave an easy victory to the aggressors. The League of Nations had the usual sessions of indecisive chatter and then finally agreed that sanctions should be applied.

The Spanish Civil War enabled foreign air units to test tactical theories. Germany in particular laid the foundation of its close support of air to ground forces which later became known as the *blitzkrieg,* and won early successes in WWII. And when the Luftwaffe destroyed Guernica in Northern Spain the Nazis demonstrated to the world not only their ruthlessness, but also what air power could and would do.

In Manchuria and China, further outrages were being committed, but the international community looked the other way. The British press and newsreels reported these atrocities and the Sunday newspapers ran features on, 'The Horrors of Air Warfare'. Film portrayed 'Things to Come'.

Alas, all these things only produced an overall feeling of helplessness and national inertia. The only economic rapid response seemed to be to order civilian gas-masks, secretly build giant crematoria and stockpile cardboard coffins.

Germany as a continental power was interested in land battles and, based on its experience in the Spanish civil war, concluded that strategic bombing from high level wasn't effective, but that by co-operation between infantry, armour and air power, quick and easy victories could be won.

19

The 'Thirties was the decade when the major countries of the world made their decisions on the type of aircraft they would fight a future war with and how they would be used in relation to the other Services.

In Germany, some of their leaders pressed for the development of four-engined bombers. These, led by Walther Werner, named Chief of Air Command Office but in reality Chief of the General Staff of the Luftwaffe, believed it better to destroy enemy weapons at source rather than on the battlefield. The result was the Ural bomber, a four-engined plane. There were also two promising prototypes ready for testing by 1936, the Junker 89 and the Dornier 19.

Werner was killed in a flying accident in June 1936 and was replaced by Herman Goering. Lt.-General Kesselring (who later became a Field Marshal) was also appointed to counterbalance the influence of Erhard Milch, 'who had for many years been building the Luftwaffe under the guise of the civil airline Lufthansa. The only matter they could agree on was that four-engined bombers were too costly in terms of raw materials and fuel consumption. Goering in April 1937 ordered heavy bombers to be scrapped. As a result Germany had no true strategic bomber in W.W.2'. [7]

Russia with the help of the Junkers Aircraft Company had the benefit of early German expertise and developed various aircraft. 'The Russian Tupolov TB3 was the four-engined monoplane bomber . . . it enabled the Red Army to form the first paratroop assault division in the world, in 1934'. [8]

In Britain expenditure was severely controlled for the Services. Although politicians talked of expansion, particularly in respect of the RAF, little was done in practical or monetary terms. Air Force Chiefs did not go for a crash programme of expansion, believing it better to have the latest aircraft, either on the drawing board or being tested as prototypes.

By 1936 the Air Ministry had laid down plans for the

future four-engined heavy strategic bomber. In line with this thinking, the light and medium bombers then coming into service were considered obsolete, as range and bombload were considered to be top priorities. The Fairey Battle, a single engine monoplane with retractable undercarriage, a range of 1,000 miles and a 1,000lb bombload, came on the scene in 1936. On, 'September 2nd 1939, 10 Battle squadrons — 160 aircraft in all — flew . . . for their new bases in France'. [9] The other bomber was the Bristol Blenheim, a twin engined monoplane with a maximum speed of 285 mph and able to carry a 1,000lb bombload as far as Germany. Initially, its only defence was a single Vickers gas operated gun! This was quickly replaced by two ·303 Browning machine-guns mounted in a turret at the rear of the pilot's cockpit which proved to be useless as defence against the cannons of the German ME109 and Focke Wolfe 190 fighters. As a result these aircraft, which did Trojan service in the early days of the war, suffered extremely heavy losses.

In 1937, the Armstrong Whitworth Whitley was introduced (nicknamed the Flying Coffin because of its silhouette) with a range of 2,400 miles, maximum speed 230 mph, an operational ceiling of 17,600ft and maximum bombload of 3,000lb. It was followed by the Handley Page Hampden (commonly called the Flying Pencil) maximum speed 265 mph at 15,000 feet and a bombload of 4,000lb. Last came the Vickers Wellington (affectionately called the Wimpy by its crews) with a range of 2,200 miles, speed 255 mph at 12,500 feet and a bombload of 1,500lb, although some publications give it a bombload of 4,000lb.

These then were the strategic bombers with which Britain commenced the air war in 1939. It was not until 1942 that the really heavy strategic bombers (first planned in 1936) appeared in the squadrons. They were the Stirling, Halifax and Manchester. The latter, put into service inadequately tested, and having killed many of its crews, was quickly withdrawn, given longer wings and four new Merlin engines to replace the two underpowered and ill-omened Vultures. It was renamed the Lancaster and soon had a new, distinctive tailplane also. It then proved to be the most outstanding bomber of the war with a range of 1,660 miles, a 14,000lb bombload, a ceiling of 24,500 ft and maximum speed of 287mph at 11,500ft. This aircraft carried the Tall Boy bomb (12,000lb) and later the Grand Slam (22,000lb) bomb.

In the USA the inter-service squabbles held back development of air power. 'In 1939 the Army Air Corp had only thirteen B17 bombers, the Flying Fortress',[10] and although its forward thinking was dedicated to daylight precision bombing, it had not considered the need to have any long-range fighter escorts.

In pre-war planning heavy bomber operations it seems obvious, even to the layman, that four basic fundamentals were not considered. Bomber aircraft had to have the range to reach the heart of the enemy and return and to be able to carry a worthwhile bombload. They had to be able to adequately defend themselves; be navigable in all weather conditions; on reaching the target be accurately able to hit it and, finally, the bombs which they dropped must have the explosive power to do the job for which they were designed.

Somehow these basic fundamentals seem to have been inadequately considered and many lives lost for nothing. The bombers that were operating at the commencement of the war did not meet all — or even most — of these criteria. They could not adequately defend themselves operating by day or by night and throughout the war were under-gunned. A fighter at night at 400 yards could stand off and use its cannon, whilst the bomber's gunners had only ·303 machine guns with which to defend their aircraft. It was only towards the end of the war when a turret using ·5 machine guns came into service, and was standard in Lincoln bombers — the aircraft to be used by the Tiger Force which joined with US in the Far East to attack Japan — that such a defence was possible.

In the early days of World War II navigators had to rely on Dead Reckoning (DR) to keep their aircraft on track to and from the target, but changes in wind speed and/or direction, which were not infrequent, could put the aircraft way off course. The only alternative to Dead Reckoning, Astro Navigation, plotting a course by the stars, was of little use when, as so often happened, the night skies were overcast by 10/10ths cloud. It was often stated that it was 'a pilot's Air Force', but the navigator played a crucial role in a bomber.

Crew members knew that although they depended on each other to survive it was on their navigator's skill they so specially had to rely. Throughout the flight as changes in wind speed, air speed, compass deviation, and drift over the earth's surface occurred and had their effect on his original course calculations, the navigator frequently had to plot and re-plot many times to ensure his aircraft remained on track to reach the target on time and, equally important, when the adrenalin had peaked, to ensure a safe return to base. It was only after three years of war that navigational aids such as Gee and H2S arrived to assist hard-pressed navigators.

Similarly, a reliable bombsight which could compensate for those evasive manoeuvres over the target which might affect accuracy was not available for service until 1942, and the bombs used by the RAF at the beginning of the war were filled with such poor explosive that they often failed to explode at all.

In wartime, all these lessons were eventually learnt and, thanks to the magnificent work of the boffins in the various Research Establishments, the early problems were overcome. But before this happened, as Charles Ashworth says, 'Shortly after taking over as C-in-C Bomber Command in October 1937, Air Chief Marshal Ludlow Hewitt had toured his Stations, and in a report a month later he did not mince his words . . . he went on to state, that Bomber Command was, 'entirely unprepared for war, unable to operate except in fair weather and extremely vulnerable both in the air and on the ground'. [11]

Inexorably in the late 'Thirties war clouds were gathering and pressure was building up on the Royal Air Force. How would it cope with the demands so soon to be made upon it?

How would it respond?

Notes, Chapter One

1. *The Air Marshals*, Allen Andrews p11
2. *The RAF in Two World Wars*, Sir Maurice Dean p33
3. *Before the Storm*, Robert Jackson p27
4. *Before the Storm*, Robert Jackson p39
5. *Before the Storm*, Robert Jackson p34
6. *The RAF in Two World Wars*, Sir Maurice Dean p39
7. *Hitler's Commanders*, Samuel W. Mitcham & Gene Mueller
8. *Guinness Book of History of Air Warfare*, D Brown, C Shores,
        K Mackey p72
9. *Before the Storm*, Robert Jackson p58
10. *The Air Marshals*, Allen Andrews p164
11. *RAF Bomber Command 1936-1968*, Chris Ashworth p10

Chapter Two

'War is the science of destruction'.

John S C Abbott

ON SEPTEMBER 1st 1939, HITLER UNLEASHED THE four Horsemen of the Apocalypse on Europe by invading Poland. At 11am on Sunday, the 3rd of September Neville Chamberlain broadcast the British declaration of war to the nation.

In the words of Webster and Frankland, 'Thus began the Bomber Command strategic air offensive against Germany. For many years it was the sole means at Britain's disposal for attacking the heart of the enemy, and, more than any other form of armed attack upon the enemy, it never ceased until almost five years later . . . It was the most continuous and gruelling operation of war ever carried out'.

Bruce Lewis describes so aptly, 'Yet from that very first day of hostilities crews were climbing into their slab-sided, matt black Armstrong Whitworth Whitleys, while others struggled to board the less cumbersome, but unbelievably cramped Handley Page Hampdens — with fuselages only three feet across at the widest point! Luckiest, from the stand point of flying the best RAF bomber then available, were those crews who manned the remarkable Vickers Wellington . . . This trio of twin-engined bombers, pitifully lacking in defensive armament, painfully slow, yet remarkably rugged, were the mainstay of Bomber Command's offensive against Germany in the early years of the war'. [1]

Bomber Command were under the strictest orders that it could only attack *ships moored in harbour or at sea*. Aircraft

25

must not attack targets on German soil. Reconnaissance flights could be made however, and propaganda leaflets dropped. These so called Nickel raids took place frequently.

The French Government's fear of large-scale reprisal raids by the German Luftwaffe was considerable and although they offered the RAF 'full facilities on French airfields it was on the understanding that its aircraft could not be used for unrestricted bombing of German targets from those bases'. [2]

Nine squadrons of Fairey Battles had flown over to France on the day before Chamberlain's broadcast. After transfers to Training Command and some squadrons of Blenheims posted to France there remained '23 operational bomber squadrons in the U.K., of which 17 were capable of making a contribution to a strategic air offensive . . . Thus apart from light bombers, Bomber Command could only field a daily force of just over 200 aircraft'. [3] Considering our obligations overseas, in the Middle East and the Far East, the RAF was more stretched than ever with old out-of-date fighter and bomber aircraft. The guardians of British interests, the politicians in Parliament had, apart from a few exceptions, betrayed not only the trust of the British people, but the citizens of the British Commonwealth and Empire.

'Following the declaration of war at 11am, at 12 noon a plane set off on the first wartime sortie to reconnoitre where warships were in the Schillig Roads of Wilhelmshaven, but with a u/s radio transmitter they returned to base and eighteen Hampdens and nine Wellingtons took off, but bad weather and the approach of darkness prevented their effort to find the ships. That same evening, on the first night operation of the war 10 Whitleys set off and, 'pushing their way through the night at all of 120mph, visited between them Hamburg, Bremen and no less than nine other cities in the Ruhr during the course of that one mission. Of course, they did not drop a single bomb on the Germans — instead they rained down 5½ million leaflets'. [4]

'RAF aircraft were not designed for comfort, and the Whitley was certainly not designed to give its crews a comfortable journey into the freezing night air over Germany. The temperature often fell to −20°. [5] It is true to say that this statement applied to most Bomber Command aircraft during WWII, even the Lancaster.

'In those earlier days of war, before the Germans had honed their night defence system into the deadly weapon that it later became, the most terrifying enemy the bomber crews had to face was the appalling weather. 1940/1941 produced the worst winter in living memory.

'The men flying the Wellingtons, Whitleys and Hampdens had to struggle through endless blankets of fog and fight fierce headwinds that reduced the forward speed of the already slow aircraft to almost nothing.

'Ice was the worst menace. It formed in thick layers on the wings. It turned hydraulic systems to jelly; gun turrets, bomb doors, undercarriages all stopped working. It formed an opaque sheen over Perspex windows, making it impossible to see out. Ice played havoc with instruments and radio. Frostbite was not uncommon among those who flew in these pioneer bombers'. [6]

'At the outbreak of war Bomber Command had three types of bombs: the 500lb GP high explosive (HE) the 250lb GP HE and the 40lb AP. All these were thick cased and stream-lined, and relied on penetration and fragmentation for their effect'.[7] They were not very effective, often failing to explode. Then again, navigation was primitive. It is one thing to fly by day and pick out landmarks, it's a different matter at night, often with thick cloud, head winds or tail winds and reliant on 'dead reckoning' which was the main navigation system at that time. Also bearing in mind the primitive and inaccurate airspeed indicator and compasses, a navigator had a very difficult job in accurately locating the target.

Unfortunately the conclusions of which Sir Edgar Ludlow-

Hewitt, AOC Bomber Command, had warned the Air Ministry by letters, memoranda and at various meetings were proving to be correct. For example, that rapid expansion would damage efficiency, that many crews were unable to find targets even in a friendly city in broad daylight and that adequate resources for training must exist. He 'repeated again his doubts as to whether his force could penetrate any distance into Germany without more protection. He even suggested that the Air Ministry should reverse its long-standing doctrine and construct long-range fighters for that purpose'. [8]

The Americans, whose crews in the so-called Flying Fortresses were to pay dearly for that omission when they came to play their part in the European war, were still ignoring the question of long-range fighter escorts.

It must not be forgotten however, that air warfare was still in its infancy and, although there was plenty of theory and certain principles had been laid down, research and development had been sorely neglected, either by oversight, lack of funds, or over confidence and failure to appreciate the operational difficulties which would occur.

The bombers ranged far and wide across Europe on leaflet raids to Prague, Vienna, Poland and many different areas of Germany. 'Leaflets would be dropped during the reconnaissance, partly for the sake of propaganda, but still more to avoid arousing the suspicions of the enemy'. [9]

Dennis Richards in his book *The Fight at Odds* says, 'Our aircraft losses over the whole period from September 1939 to 6th April 1940 — six per cent of sorties engaged primarily on pamphlet-dropping — were certainly far too expensive for any immediate effect achieved on the enemy . . . From this experience emerged improvements of the highest value. New devices for ensuring the well-being of aircrews at high altitudes; better arrangements for landing and ditching in emergency, and for escaping from the aircraft: the development of navigational aids; these were but part of the legacy from the pioneers who bombed Germany with paper'. [10]

The contributions of those that flew the Bristol Blenheim and the Fairey Battle should not be overlooked. The former generally flew during daylight. 'The crews of the Blenheims,' said Bruce Lewis, 'kept up an unremitting attack on enemy-occupied channel ports and targets near the coast. Any gentlemanly agreements relating to bomber restrictions had come to an end when the Germans bombed Rotterdam on 15th May 1940. During the Battle of Britain, Blenheim Squadrons played a vital role . . . They, and the Wellingtons destroyed hundreds of motorised barges concentrated by the enemy'.[11] In discussing the Fairey Battle, he goes on to say, 'the courage of the crews who flew to their deaths in Battles has never been fully acknowledged. In the Spring of 1940, when the Germans invaded the Low Countries, the Advanced Air Striking Force was thrown into the battle to try and stem the enemy onslaught . . . The losses among the Battles and Blenheims reached horrific proportions. They were shot out of the sky, either by withering fire from mobile flak batteries, or as a result of relentless attacks by Messerschmitt 109 fighters, whose superior fire power and speed left the Battles, in particular, with almost no hope of survival'. [12]

With the French still persisting in restricting bombing mainland Germany, 'Americans watching, from comfortable seats outside the arena the cautious sparring and pulled punches of the opposing heavyweights, dismissed the contest as phoney. The epithet was hardly justified. One of the contestants was nursing his strength for the later stages of the fight; the other was about to launch an all-out effort in the next round. Certainly there was nothing 'phoney' about the war for our aircrews, despite the strong restrictions on bombing observed by both sides. For restrictions or no restrictions, our airmen had still to drone their way over Germany through night and the enemy defences, or ceaselessly scan the wastes of ocean, or to speed to combat with the molester of our shipping, or — and this to most was the true hardship — sit long, bitter hours at dispersal, waiting for the call that did not come'. [13] The term phoney was now dropped from reporting, for the German forces were again ready to march. In early April 1940, Norway and Denmark were invaded and soon overrun. Bomber Command commenced new forms of anti-shipping operations. The terms 'Vegetables' and 'Gardening' entered the airman's vocabulary. These terms were used when aircraft dropped mines off the coast of Denmark and other areas that would cause maximum mayhem to enemy shipping. 'As the war proceeded, the plain acoustic and plain magnetic mines were combined in proportions which constantly varied, thus setting the enemy a difficult, and, as time went on, an insoluble problem in his attempts to sweep them'. [14]

On 2nd April 1940, ACM Ludlow-Hewitt was relieved from his position as AOC-in C Bomber Command, a position he had held since 1937. Like Dowding later, the powers-that-be decided he should be removed, probably because he had constantly pointed out that his Command was not up to the job for which it had been created. However in his new post as Inspector-General, he was able to use both his technical and practical knowledge to the benefit of the Service.

The new AOC-in C Bomber Command was Air-Marshal Charles Portal. When he took over, his forces amounted to only, '15 Squadrons, totalling about 240 aircraft of which about 160 would be available at any one time'. [15]

Events were now moving swiftly. On May 10th 1940, Winston Churchill took over the direction of Britain's affairs, and on the same day the German forces began the invasion of the Low Countries. On 14th May, Rotterdam was all but destroyed and the 15th saw all Dutch resistance collapse, 'Bomber Command was authorised to attack East of the Rhine and that night ninety-nine bombers were despatched to attack oil and railway targets in the Ruhr'. [16] So the Bomber Command strategic air offensive against Germany got under way.

With the German columns swiftly advancing into France, plans were put in hand for the possible evacuation of the British Expeditionary Force. On 27th May these were put into effect and the Dunkirk evacuation commenced. Some 338,226 men were taken off the beaches and the whole operation largely completed by 4th June. The RAF played a vital role that was not always appreciated by those on the ground, 'Dunkirk, like the operations which preceded it, was for the Royal Air Force a battle of arms — not, as is sometimes imagined, an affair of fighters alone. The fighters indeed bore the main share by covering the bridgeheads and the sea-lanes, but we must remember, too, the reconnaissance aircraft which brought back details of the military position and kept watch against U-boats and E-boats, and bombers which harassed and held up any troops and silenced vital batteries'. [17]

After the successful evacuation from France of British and Allied troops, the tide of events moved with steady but relentless pressure against British interests. Italy declared war on France and Britain, and was making plans to attack Yugoslavia and Greece in addition to enlarging its North African Empire. Russia annexed the Baltic States and the Northern Provinces of Roumania. In France the continuing success of the German Army brought about a second evacuation and finally the Petain Government sought an armistice which was signed on 22nd June 1940. Whilst these events were unfolding, the RAF Bomber Offensive targeted Turin, Genoa and Milan.

Attacks upon Germany were increasing steadily. Hitler believed Britain would sue for peace, but ostensibly had plans prepared for an invasion. Barges and other vessels began to appear in increasing numbers at ports in Holland, Belgium and France. Bomber Command proceeded to attack and sink them, whilst continuing to carry out the task of mining enemy waters.

Throughout, Churchill knew from the enemy intercepts privately relayed from Bletchley Park that a seaborne invasion was most unlikely. He nevertheless kept this information to himself, to stiffen the urgency of British resistance. He knew the strategy was needed and, in time, it worked.

'The Command entered upon the campaign in May, 1940 as a weak under-strength force; it would stand at the end of the offensive in May 1945 as the most powerful striking force in all British history. Its five years campaign would end in doubt and bitter controversy'. [18] A steady stream of directives was being sent by Air Ministry to Portal at High Wycombe during this period, constantly changing areas of attack until he complained and criticised the strategy.

In August the Command's aircraft made the first of several attacks on Berlin in retaliation for enemy bombs dropped on London. The defences of Britain were being tested by the Luftwaffe in raids that would increase in strength and savagery against airfields and, later, against towns and cities. On 3rd Sept, 1940, Churchill wrote a paper to the War Cabinet stating, 'The Navy can lose us the war, but only the Air Force can win it . . . The fighters are our salvation, but the bombers alone can provide the means of victory . . . The Air Force and its action on the largest scale must therefore claim the first place over the Navy or the Army'. [19] 'Churchill followed this policy statement with a memo suggesting that the RAF should spread its bombs as widely as possible over the cities of Germany'. [20]

The first sustained enemy attack, 'heavy and deliberate . . was delivered against London on the afternoon and night of Saturday 7th September, 1940 involving nearly 600 bombers, ten times as many as the RAF had sent against Berlin. The

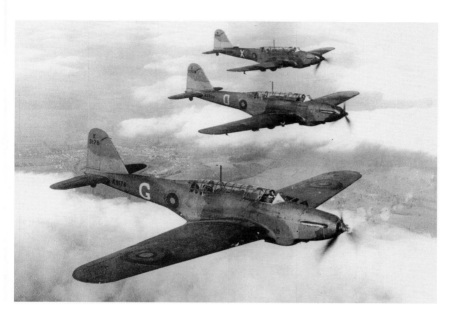

THE FAIREY BATTLE
Light Bomber

THE HANDLEY PAGE HAMPDEN
Medium Bomber

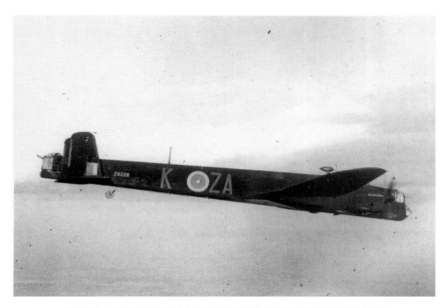

THE ARMSTRONG WHITWORTH WHITLEY
Heavy Bomber

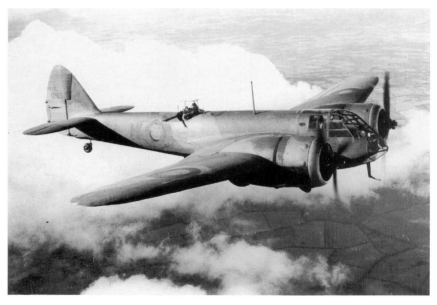

THE BRISTOL BLENHEIM
Light Medium Bomber

Blitz had begun. It was to continue almost every night until May 1941, with occasional diversions to the major cities. The result, unforeseen by Bomber Command was to give Fighter Command the respite it so desperately needed, for the potentially decisive daylight attacks on its airfields ceased'. [21] The RAF's attack on Berlin had so enraged Hitler that he had ordered the Luftwaffe to switch its assault on airfields to the bombardment of London.

Fighter Command had won the Battle of Britain and Churchill's, 'Never has so much been owed by so many to so few', brilliantly summed up the nation's gratitude to those pilots who fought so magnificently and so selflessly over the fields of southern England. Nevertheless Bomber Command also made its contribution by continuously attacking the German invasion fleet assembling across the Channel. 'Between 15 July and 21 September RAF Bomber Command — according to German naval sources — sank or damaged 21 transports and 214 barges in Channel ports, some 12 per cent of the total invasion fleet'. [22] Bomber Command now pursued its own plans for bombing German targets. The odds were stacked against the crews. 'The aircraft were fitted with inadequate ancillary equipment; the only navigational aid the navigator was supplied with was a sextant. The a/c were without heating and the cold was appalling, the crews flew clothed in layers of silk, wool and leather and yet they were bitterly cold. Vital systems jammed, wings iced up for the lack of adequate de-icing gear, guns froze and the crews' limbs seized with cold'. [23] Despite this, with most aircraft except perhaps the Wellington under-gunned, the aircrews strove mightily to carry out their task.

On October 4th Sir Cyril Newall, the Chief of Air Staff retired and Sir Charles Portal took his place, taking with him to Whitehall, as Deputy Chief of the Air Staff, 'his most dynamic Group Commander, Arthur Harris, who had previously served there . . . . in the Plans Directorate . . . he left the Air Ministry in May 1941 for an appointment overseas'. [24]

The new AOC-in-C Bomber Command was Sir Richard Pierce. Under his stewardship the bomber crews continued their allotted tasks as laid down by the Air Ministry directives.

Robert Jackson tells of the coming into service of the Boeing Fortress 1's, which had been offered by the US government to the British Purchasing Commission. It was hoped by using these aircraft precision daylight operations from high altitude could be carried out. It would appear they were not successful and he concludes, 'There was no escaping the fact that as a high altitude day bomber the Fortress 1 had fallen far short of expectations'. [25] Modifications in later marks of the airplane, when it was the mainstay of the US Army Air Forces attacking force in Europe, finally proved it a winner.

From the British point of view, if they were to continue to carry the war to the enemy night operations were the only option. However doubts were now being raised that many of the crews were not dropping their bombs in the right places. When photographic reconnaissance was undertaken by specially modified high flying Spitfires, the results of bombing operations were damaging. The Butt report, which covered assessment of one month's bombing operations, was issued in August 1941 and concluded, 'that of those crews recorded as attacking their targets only one in three got within 5 miles, the remainder of the bomb loads being dropped on the wrong target, in open country, or the excellent decoys provided by the Germans'. [26] This report caused considerable heart searching in many quarters but it underlined the urgent need to improve navigation, which included producing good navigation aids and target-finding and marking equipment.

In July 1941 Bomber Command was instructed to direct the efforts of the bomber force to attacking the German transportation system, with the secondary aim of destroying civilian morale. This latter part of the directive would seem to have caused some historians, including the authors of *The Strategic Air Offensive against Germany*, Sir Charles Webster and Dr Noble Frankland, to say, 'Sir Charles Portal believed the time had come to attack the German people'. This was not the case, rather that Portal felt that it was better to bomb any target in an industrial area than have the crews risk their lives needlessly. Bomber Command had tried precision bombing since the start of the war, but had not been successful for reasons stated earlier. The Luftwaffe in that same period had ruthlessly bombed Warsaw, Rotterdam, many British cities, and Belgrade where after three days of continuous assault over 17,000 civilians died.

When the question of morality is raised, the short answer is that all war is immoral. All the inhabitants of any town which refused to surrender to Genghis Khan were slaughtered, men, women, children — even babies. In Napoleonic times if a Spanish city under siege and did not surrender, when the final assault took place and entry was gained, conquering troops looted, raped and murdered for two or three days before order could be restored. Surely not only 'immoral' acts, but ones of satanic evil. Where is the morality in the use of flame-throwers or napalm? Mankind throughout history has not yet solved its disagreements by discussion — only by fighting. The simple truth is that compared to the 'sophisticated' long range electronically guided weapons of this atomic age World War II weapons were clumsy and crude. Lessons were being learnt as the war progressed and laid the foundations of today's unprecedented accuracy.

'Though critics tended to regard 'destroying morale' as a euphemism for 'killing', it was no part of the policy deliberately to slaughter civilians. Heavy casualties would inevitably be involved, — but the primary intention was to make it difficult or impossible for civilians, many of whom were an essential part of the war machine, to remain at their industrial or administrative jobs'. [27]

Von Clausewitz has said, 'kind hearted people might, of course think there is some ingenious way to disarm or defeat the enemy without too much bloodshed, and might imagine this to be a true goal of the art of war. Pleasant as it sounds, it is a fallacy that must be exposed. War is such a dangerous business that the mistakes which come from kindness are the very worst'.

The bomber was the only way open to us at that time to take the war to the enemy.

The stark reality facing Britain at that time was that on almost every front where war was being waged, the news was of setbacks and defeats. The Balkans overrun; Greece having to surrender; the loss of Crete and the endless battles of our armies in the Western Desert; the U-boat menace in the Atlantic. All these matters confronted the Chiefs of Staff and the War Cabinet who had to make difficult decisions and didn't have the luxury of hindsight. In addition to the above there were the reports of the suffering of the people of the countries now under Nazi occupation. An untold number of those people were dragged from their homes and used as forced labour in Nazi controlled war industries, thereby filling the gaps created by the conscription of more men to fight on the Russian front. Meantime reports were being received of the ill treatment of Jews throughout Hitler's Europe leading on to the hideous atrocity of the Holocaust.

Britain had at that time no realistic chance of returning to Europe with an Army. How then was she to cause havoc and disruption to the enemy's war machine, or tie up men and production vitally needed on the Russian front? The future was indeed bleak. The British Army was neutralised and short of weapons. The Navy had its hands full to keep the vital shipping lanes open, battling against the U-boats and German air attacks at sea. To the War Cabinet, Bomber

36

Command was the only Force available to contain the enemy's expanding war-making potential, both in weaponry and labour which eventually 'rose to 7½ million foreign and prisoners of war in the labour force'.[28]

New heavy four engined bombers were soon to come into service with the Squadrons. Work at Defence Research Establishments was to bear fruit, particularly in the field of navigation. First was Gee followed by H2S, which would enable crews to locate their targets; then bigger and more efficient bombs, aimed with greater accuracy using the new bombsights and, finally, a change in command. Sir Richard Pierce was to be replaced. 'He was a victim of circumstances. He had presided over the fortunes of Bomber Command when they were at their lowest ebb, when bomber crews paid with their lives for the short-sighted politicians and reduced standards of training brought about by decisions taken in previous years. He had been blamed for policy decisions that were none of his doing, such as the drain of vital aircraft and crews from Bomber Command to reinforce squadrons in the Middle East. Mistakes and fundamental errors of judgement he had certainly made, but then so had others in higher authority'. [29] He paid the price. A new commander was to take over.

During the Washington Conference in December 1941, Portal offered Harris — who was heading the RAF delegation to the United States — the post of AOC-in-C, Bomber Command. Harris accepted and would remain in post for the duration of the war. All the wealth of experience gained from the positions he had held during and since WWI had had a profound influence on both his thinking and the way in which he intended to wage the air war.

His was a very lonely position. All supreme commanders know Harry Truman's dictum, 'The buck stops here'. However, for Harris, it was considerably more difficult. Firstly, he was in many ways pioneering the theory and

37

practice of aerial warfare. Secondly, unlike a Commander-in-Chief in the other Services, once he had assessed the situation and had a firm grip on his Command, weather permitting he invariably committed the whole of the bomber force into battle, the loss of which would have left this country without the means of attacking the enemy's homeland.

Arthur Travers Harris was not a fool and he did not suffer fools gladly. When he was the Deputy Chief of Air Staff he cleared out many of the hangers-on and paper shufflers at Air Ministry whose self-importance caused them 'to blow themselves up with the full authority of the Air Council'. [30] He was blunt, often accused of rudeness, of explosive temperament and had great energy. He would argue strongly for what he believed, but if he was over-ruled he would devote the whole of his energies to carry out his instructions to the best of his ability.

A typical example is when the formation of the Pathfinder Force was mooted, which will be referred to later.

Like many other Commanders of whatever Service or whatever country, he was human and obviously fallible. He had his critics both during and after the war. It was said that when Harris was on a buying mission in America, his blunt manner upset the sensibilities of the U.S. Generals, but this, subsequently, has been denied.

When the anniversary of the bombing of Dresden comes round the media has generally repeated the myths that Harris was responsible for 'area bombing' and thus the decision to bomb and virtually obliterate the city. It usually manages to include propaganda from previous enemy sources that Bomber Harris and his crews should be indicted as war criminals. Max Hastings states, 'Yet Harris's style, the stories about his rudeness and extravagance contributed immensely to his popularity with his overwhelmingly lower middle-class bomber crews. They endeared him to them, though they never saw him . . . Harris was a real leader from beginning to end in seeming to identify himself totally with the interests of his men'. [31]

In contrast Wilber H Morrison writes, 'Harris was a disciplined man, heavy set and of medium height and handsome. He was reserved, but his subordinates quickly learned that his tremendous energy and scathing denunciation of inadequacy made him a difficult boss. He had no tolerance for failures if he thought they could be avoided. Once he made a decision, his instructions were precise and he insisted they be carried out to the letter. If they weren't, staff officers in particular received the full benefit of a voice that could cut like a whiplash'. [32]

Unlike Field Marshal Montgomery who made a point of travelling around constantly to address his troops and explain his plans, Harris was a remote figure at High Wycombe, rarely visiting his squadrons. Even so, he was generally known throughout his Command as 'Butch', short for Butcher; not as some of his detractors have said because of the results of the raids carried out by his crews, or because of his insensitivity to the loss of bomber crews on operations; instead it was an example of the black humour of his men, who recognised he spared no one, and would continue sending them to their deaths as long as events dictated.

Moreover, unlike most senior officers, Harris was indifferent to personal publicity. He said, 'I considerably annoyed many representatives of the press by refusing to see them or hold press conferences'. [33] This may account for the bad press he has had from time to time. He was always a controversial figure. Nevertheless he 'was indeed a most sensitive and humane man. He made an admirable partner with the Americans. His robust, forthright and intensively practical approach removed all risk of doubt or hesitation, as the United States found out in the strategic air offensive against Germany'. [34]

Much has been written about the issue of area bombing.

It has frequently been suggested that it was instituted by Harris when he became Bomber Chief. Strangely the same charge was made against Portal when he took over Bomber Command. The Official Historians, Sir Charles Webster and Dr Noble Frankland say, 'Bomber Command as represented by its Commander-in-Chief Sir Charles Portal now believed that this by-product should become an end itself. He believed the time had come to launch a direct attack on the German people themselves'. [35]

The widening of bombing policy from purely military targets actually came in a directive which awaited Harris when he took over command at High Wycombe. It authorised the employment of the resources under his command without restriction and that aiming points could be built up areas. Many writers give the impression that this meant that Herr Schmidt of 10 Finkelstrasse was to be the aiming point or, the watchmaker in some other Strasse in a German city. They labour under the delusion that Harris instituted the area bombing policy, choosing to ignore the fact it was already in force. Harris stated in his book, 'There is a widespread impression, which has often got into print, that I not only invented the policy of area bombing but also insisted on carrying it out in the face of the natural reluctance to kill women and children that was felt by everyone else. The facts are otherwise. Such decisions of policy are not in any case made by Commanders-in-Chief in the field but by Ministries, by the Chiefs of Staff Committee and by the War Cabinet'. [36]

He might well have added: 'Ultimately by Winston Churchill, the Prime Minister'.

Air Marshal Harris headed Bomber Command on 22nd February 1942, just seven weeks before his 50th birthday. In the First World War he had been commissioned in the Royal Flying Corp, seen action as a fighter pilot on the Western Front and returned to England to command a home defence unit. He was a pioneer night fighter pilot and was awarded the AFC in November 1918. Given a permanent position with the rank of Squadron Leader in 1921, he commanded a Squadron in India, then moved to air policing in Iraq. Whilst serving in the Middle East he pioneered the prone position for bomb aiming.

Through the locust years he went to Army Staff College and was an instructor. He went from there to Air Ministry as Deputy Director of Ops and Intelligence, and then became head of Air Ministry Planning Department until 1938. In that position he pointed out, 'the target would need to be marked by some form of long-burning pyrotechnic device, but before the war began no effective flares had been designed, much less ordered, and the use of those which did exist was discouraged'. [37]

Allen Andrews said, 'Bomber Harris has claimed credit for many facets of the final air victory, but he has never publicly mentioned the memorandum of 16 January 1935 drawn up by Group Captain A. T. Harris Deputy Director of Plans, advocating a policy of building aircraft of maximum range and bomb capacity so that even the medium bombers would disappear. His advocacy, which was not unsupported, was effective'. [38]

In 1937 he was Commander of No.4 Group, flying Whitleys, the only group at the time to specialise in night bombing. After a year he was promoted to Air Vice-Marshal to command the RAF in Palestine and Transjordan. In 1938 he led the RAF Purchasing Mission to the US and a week after the outbreak of war he became AOC 5 Group and initiated the Hampden mining campaign, the forerunner of the successful mining operations which had such dire results on German shipping during the war. The Group also contributed to the bombing of the invasion barges assembling in the Chanel ports.

In November 1940 he was summoned by Portal, who was now Chief of Air Staff, to become his Deputy Chief at the

Air Ministry, but Portal subsequently felt obliged to send him back to America as Head of the RAF Delegation to Washington.

Whilst there, Portal invited him to take over as C-in-C, Bomber Command, which he accepted and the post in which he remained until the war's end. He was a truly experienced all-rounder, who was chosen to carry out the policies of the War Cabinet conducting the air war, and in controlling the bomber force at most critical time in the war in Europe.

Notes, Chapter Two

1. *Aircrew*, Bruce Lewis p3 & 4
2. *Before the Storm*, Robert Jackson p57
3. *RAF Bomber Command 1936-1968*, Chris Ashworth p23
4. *Aircrew*, Bruce Lewis p4
5. *The Six-Year Offensive*, Ken Delve & Peter Jacobs p30
6. *Aircrew*, Bruce Lewis p7
7. *Bomber Harris*, Charles Messenger p30
8. *The Strategic Air Offensive Against Germany Vol 1*, Webster
    & N Frankland p96
9. *The RAF 1939/45 Vol 1*, Denis Richards p53
10. *The RAF 1939/45 Vol 1*, Denis Richards p54
11. *Aircrew*, Bruce Lewis p8
12. *Aircrew*, Bruce Lewis p9
13. *The RAF 1939/45 Vol 1*, Denis Richards p69 & 70
14. *The RAF 1939/45 Vol 3*, Hilary St G Saunders p16
15. *The Bombers*, Norman Longmate p84
16. *The Strategic Air Offensive Against Germany Vol 1*,

Webster & Frankland p144

17. *The RAF 1939/45 Vol 1*, Denis Richards p130 & 131
18. *Uncommon Valour*, AG Goulding p32
19. *The Bombers*, Norman Longmate p88
20. *RAF Bomber Command 1936-1968*, Chris Ashworth p99
21. *The Bombers*, Norman Longmate p89
22. *Before the Storm*, Robert Jackson p129
23. *Uncommon Valour*, AG Goulding p36
24. *The Bombers*, Norman Longmate p91
25. *Before the Storm*, Robert Jackson p154
26. *RAF Bomber Command 1936-1968*, Chris Ashworth p51
27. *The Hardest Victory*, Denis Richards p86
28. *The Strategic Air Offensive Against Germany Vol 1*,
        Webster & Frankland p277
29. *Before the Storm*, Robert Jackson p175 & 176
30. *Bomber Offensive*, Sir Arthur Harris p49
31. *Bomber Command*, Max Hastings p161
32. *Fortress Without a Roof*, Wilbur H Morrison p21
33. *Bomber Offensive*, Sir Arthur Harris p119
34. *The Royal Air Force in Two World Wars*, Sir Maurice Dean
        p310 & 311
35. *Uncommon Valour*, AG Goulding p39
36. *Bomber Offensive*, Sir Arthur Harris p88
37. *The Bombers*, Norman Longmate p55
38. *The Air Marshals*, Allen Andrews p51

Chapter Three

'We cannot make war as we ought, we can only make it as we can.'

Lord Kitchener

THE NEW C-IN-C TOOK OVER ON FEBRUARY 22nd 1942
and inherited a frontline strength of about 400 bombers, 'At
the beginning of March 1942 Harris commanded only 44½
operational squadrons, with another 8½ non-operational. Of
the operational squadrons, 11 so far had the new 'heavies'. In
terms of aircraft actually available with crews, Harris could
rely in 1942 on an average nightly total of only about 350
suitable for operations over Germany'. [1]

But fortunately he did have that element of luck, so
essential to anyone who is to be successful. The new
Lancaster bomber was coming into service, 'Its efficiency was
almost incredible, both in performance and in every way it
could be saddled with ever increasing loads without breaking
the camel's back. It is astonishing that so small an aircraft as
the Lancaster could so easily take the enormous 22,000 lb
'Grand Slam' bomb, a weapon which no other aircraft in the
world could as yet carry. The Lancaster far surpassed any
other type of heavy bomber'. [2]

New navigational aids, so desperately needed by the
bomber crews, were about to appear on the scene. As was a
new force to ensure targets were correctly identified and —
with the aide of new devices — accurately hit. Names such as
Gee, the new radar navigational aid; H2S, a bombing aid
which showed outlines of the target on a screen and then
Oboe, a blind bombing device. The use of these navigational
aids greatly improved the Pathfinder's technique of marking

targets (with a range reaching to the Ruhr). As it was able to rise to 30,000ft or more the Mosquito aircraft was used by the Pathfinder Force since the efficiency of the equipment was dependent upon the altitude of the aircraft using it. In addition the new Mark XIV bombsight came into operation, which was, according to Harris, 'far more efficient'. Ultimately the appointment of a Master Bomber to direct each raid helped to ensure the accuracy of both the marking and bombing of the target.

'Far more damaging to the Bomber's efforts than the claims of the Army was the claim of the Navy, which persistently called upon Bomber Command for action against enemy shipping and naval dockyards, neither of which were easy targets; sea mining, invasion barges, naval raiders at sea or in dock and protected shelters for submarines were destructible only by direct hits with specialised bombs and were well protected by A.A. guns'. [3] The deep penetration bomb was yet to come.

In the wider world, a series of events now occurred which initially made the future seem even darker and more threatening than ever. On December 7th, without any declaration of war, the Japanese attacked and sank a large part of the United States Pacific Fleet in Pearl Harbour and, on the very next day invaded British Malaya and sank two British battleships, HMS *Repulse* and *Prince of Wales*.

The Japanese invasion of the Philippines followed and the surrender of Hong Kong accompanied by hideous Japanese atrocities. The Solomon Islands and New Guinea were next to be invaded, posing a real threat of an assault on Australia. The one bright spark to show through the gloom of disaster was that the US was now firmly committed to fight with Britain against Japanese aggression in the Far East and the Pacific and also — but only after Hitler declared war on the US in support of his Far Eastern ally — Nazi Germany too.

The massive industrial capacity and know-how of the

United States was now finally committed to the Allied cause, but even that had its downside. America had been slumbering, despite all the efforts of President Theodore Roosevelt, whilst German armies smashed their way across Europe.

At last awakened to the global peril which Britain had perceived in 1939 — or, in the case of Winston Churchill, even earlier — a navy had to be re-equipped and enlarged; an army enlisted, trained and equipped from a few thousands to over a million in well under a year; and an Army Corps provided with machines which, a few months earlier, might have been on the RAF's shopping list.

To the British people the constant stream of setbacks plus serious U-boat sinkings in the battle of the Atlantic was causing great anxiety, making it all the more important to raise morale and to carry on no matter how grave the outlook seemed. Churchill did much to boost the spirit of the nation with his wartime speeches. Taking all this into consideration, there really was no alternative open to the Joint Chiefs and the War Cabinet other than using Bomber Command to carry the war to the enemy by destroying its war-making potential. Disagreements in some circles were surfacing. The other Services still wanted the resources to Bomber Command cut and to have their air-arms returned to them, particularly as they were sure that the inability of the bombers to locate and hit their targets showed that money could be better spent on their respective Service requirements. It was also felt that the high losses among bomber crews indicated they should have been better deployed. Churchill seemed to be blowing hot and cold over the possibilities of the strategic air offensive. Members of Parliament were questioning the policy and some leading Churchmen argued about the morality of aerial bombardment itself.

It was against this background that Harris took over his Command: exactly the right man in the right place at the right time. For it truly needed a commander of great experience with nerves of steel and unswerving determination to prove to the doubters what Bomber Command was capable of and what would be achieved. Only a few days before his arrival at High Wycombe, 3 German battleships, *Gneisenau, Scharnhorst* and *Prince Eugen* had made a daylight dash to safer havens in German ports. Although Bomber Command had aircraft on standby, the prevailing weather at take-off prevented some crews from sighting the ships, whilst others were unable to attack because of the low cloud base.

Not that the ships escaped unscathed. Mines previously laid by Bomber Command caused serious damage to the *Scharnhorst* and the *Gneisenau* on the 1st stage of their run for the Elbe. 'It meant the end of the raids on Brest which had cost the Command 127 aircraft and diverted much effort from the attack on Germany'. [4]

Weather was a constant problem, with bad cloud conditions, wind variations, icing, or all three, particularly during the winter months. When the target was found, especially in the case of the Reich, industrial haze frequently obscured the aiming point, and often dummy fires were lit in open country to confuse and mislead the bomb aimers. Those early years of 1940 and 1941 were particularly hard on the crews flying in unheated aircraft with temperatures sometimes as low as minus 30 degrees with heavy icing on the wings and having to endure flights of up to eight hours or more. It was so different for the German aircrews based just across the Channel. Ours had to travel across the North Sea and France, or Holland or Denmark before they could reach German territory.

'In the course of late 1940 and 1941 General Kammhuber, in charge of the force, built up around the frontiers open to RAF penetration, from Denmark through to Holland, a system of interception zones'. [5]

Later the zones almost extended to Paris in the south. 'In

the RAF, though not in Germany, this was known as the Kammhuber Line. The forward zone was divided into 'boxes' in each of which were stationed one early warning *Freya* radar and two close range *Würzburg* radars. After the *Freya* had first picked up the incoming bombers one of the *Würzburgs* plotted it, while the other plotted the intercepting fighter. A controller on the ground with both displays before him could direct the fighter by R/T into the vicinity of the bomber.

'If the bomber penetrated through this radar zone he then came into a searchlight zone, later also assisted by radar, where the fighter could continue his attack. In either case there was no "friendly" flak to disturb the fighter'. [6]

'Night fighters who approached the anti-aircraft "boxes" — areas in which the guns were concentrated so as to cover a fixed section of the sky — were required to fly above 18,000 ft to avoid interfering with their own flak'. [7]

'By January 1942 the total number of flak guns had almost doubled to 4,416 heavy and 7,454 medium light guns, supported by 3,276 searchlights'. [8]

Later in the war heavy concentrations of anti-aircraft guns were to surround the German industries in the Ruhr and the big cities. 'The Germans employed 3 types of heavy Flak, 88mm, 105mm and 128mm — and two types of light Flak — 20mm and 37mm. The light guns, of which, more than 2,200 were deployed in the West, fired a great deal of tracer, usually referred to by the bomber crews as 'Flaming Onions' and were largely ineffective against Lancasters and Halifaxes at their normal operating heights. The 37mm Flak could, however, reach the Stirling. Of the heavy guns, by far the most numerous were the 88mm, which formed the core of the German Flak defences. Of the 11,000 heavy Flak guns deployed in the West were the 88mm Type 36. These guns . . . fired a shell weighing 18lb to a height that brought all three types of heavy bomber well within their range'. [9]

48

How the German armies fighting on the Russian Front would have liked to have wrested these 88's away from the defences against Bomber Command and had them as much-needed anti-tank weapons.

'By the autumn of 1943 the Germans were using almost 7,000 searchlights in the west. These were of two main types, usually referred to by the bomber crews as 'Masters' and 'Slaves' . . . Because of the types employed, the Masters appeared to generate a blue-tinged light, while the Slaves generated a white light. The beams of the Master searchlights usually pointed upwards or were doused until their controlling radar had located a target aircraft. The Master would then immediately illuminate the target and the Slave lights would attempt to 'cone' it . . .

'Apart from illuminating individual aircraft, the searchlights were also used to assist single-seater fighters by illuminating the clouds to provide a background against which the bombers could be silhouetted'. [10]

These were the formidable defences, in addition to the weather, which confronted the crews as they set out into the darkness each night. On a moonless night the ground below was dark, yet to look up, the sky was illuminated by starlight and sometimes the silhouette of another bomber might briefly come into view, vanishing as quickly as it appeared. Or a sudden lurch could be experienced if crossing the slipstream of another aircraft. On the wings, the exhausts from the engines glowed red as they belched flames — something that would not be seen looking out of a porthole in one of today's aircraft, so comfortable with its air-conditioning.

When the moon was up it brightened the surrounding sky and, looking below the aircraft, there were nights when the clouds appeared like wisps of cotton-wool, on others, a complete blanket of cloud on which a silhouette of the aircraft rode silently.

The crew were always busy with their individual tasks.

The rear-gunner felt seemingly suspended in space, travelling backwards, only assured he was attached to the plane as he swivelled his turret from side to side searching the sky. A few yards down the fuselage the mid-upper gunner's turret was situated: a large Perspex cupola which stuck out of the top of the aircraft. He had the best view of all with a full 360° turret rotation — enabling him to check the underside of the aircraft as it made a gentle bank from side to side, ensuring no enemy fighter was sneaking up beneath it with its lethal vertical cannon. A strip of canvas was his seat and three or four feet below the turret was the thin metal skin of the plane.

Just aft was the bomb bay with its deadly cargo. Forward of the main spar, sat the wireless operator busy listening to his set and just forward of him, curtained off to hide even the lowest glimmer of light, sat the navigator with his maps and charts. Near him was the bomb aimer (acting as second navigator) who worked the navigation aids, Gee and H2S.

In the nose of the aircraft, on the port side of the cockpit, was the pilot — the only man to have a small piece of armour plating behind his head. He, regardless of his rank or the ranks of other members of his crew, was always 'The Skipper': always the commander of the aircraft. Next to him, on the starboard side, was the flight engineer constantly checking banks of dials. The loneliest posts were those of the gunners who were virtually encased in their tiny turrets, with only their thoughts as company as they manipulated the handlebar triggers which swung their turrets from side to side, enabling them to search the darkened sky for friend or foe. Although the members of the crew were linked by intercom, it was only to be used for passing information to each other, not idle chatter.

A typical night's Maximum Effort raid over enemy occupied Europe would commence with the Squadrons setting out from Yorkshire, Lincolnshire, Cambridgeshire and Norfolk, all making for the rendezvous of the Bomber Stream, often Beachy Head, on the south coast, if the target was in Southern Germany and to The Wash, on the east coast, for North German targets.

It was a common sight to see navigation lights of assembling bombers begin to appear all over the evening sky; later to see them suddenly disappear, as if a master-switch had been pressed, when they reached the coast. The aircraft now began to form a wide stream as they crossed the sea, steadily climbing to operational height as they headed towards Germany. Having crossed the enemy coast, sometimes in the distance, north or south of the track, the darkness of the night sky might be illuminated by the pencils of white light thrown up by searchlights, wavering to and fro and often followed by the flicker of gunfire and a sudden blossom of flame, indicating that some poor chap had strayed off course and 'bought it'.

As the first of the bombers approached the target area, searchlights would begin to criss-cross the sky and, as the ghostly light of flares lit up the ground below and the Pathfinders released their Target Indicators (T.I.s), the first bursts of flak would explode in the sky.

The colour of the T.I.s, which were changed nightly to prevent the enemy putting up dummies, appeared to drip slowly earthward, marking the aiming point for the Main Force of bombers to hit with their incendiaries and high explosive. With the raid well under way the orangey-red of spreading fires would be blotted out by the haze of drifting smoke, through which brilliant exploding flashes of 'Cookies', 4,000lb bombs could be seen.

By this time the sky would be streaked with coloured tracer from the flak batteries below, which appeared to rise very slowly and then accelerate past the bombers, coupled with deep black blobs of the heavy flak and the rattle of shrapnel playing against the fuselages of the aircraft. A scene from Dante's *Inferno* comes to mind. To the crews, the only sound was the drone of the engines which held them aloft.

A sudden jolt of the aircraft was felt as the bombs were released. The aircraft lifted. Anxious moments passed as the pilot maintained straight and level flight whilst the telltale camera took photographs of the bomb plot. At last, after what seemed an age, the bomb-aimer's voice came over the intercom, 'Bomb doors closed', and the aircraft could turn away to seek the welcome cloak of darkness and head for home.

On departure from the target area the ground beneath appeared to be a scintillating mixture of rippling colour, like jewellery caught up in the rays of light, ruby red, emerald green sparkling in a sea of fire from which further diamond bright flashes of the exploding bombs would occur from more incoming bombers. 'A crew still faced the long flight home, it was then that most losses occurred, some aircraft were damaged, pilots were tired and the night fighters had had time to assemble for the kill'. [11] When they eventually arrived back at their bases, they would taxi to the dispersal points, shut down the engines and crews would emerge, usually into the cold pre-dawn morning, tired but pleased for it was one more 'Op' to count towards the final tally of a completed tour or tours.

Strangely, it was nearly always the first and last trip that stuck in the memory. The first because despite the uncertainty there was a mixture of excitement and fear of the unknown, to experience at first-hand what this flying on operations was all about.

The last was different because the previously unknown was now known only too well, it had been experienced many times. It needs to be remembered that a 'tour' of operations was usually a minimum of 30 operations and it was not unheard of for some to fly two, three or in rare cases even four tours, and the last operation could so easily be your turn to become a casualty of war.

Aircrews did break the inexorable pattern, of course, by having leaves or 48 hour passes. If the Squadron was 'stood down' for a day or, if having been briefed the operaton was 'scrubbed', cancelled at the last minute, the crews would rush back to the billets, change uniforms and make for the nearest village or town. Such visits usually resulted in high jinks, causing some locals to talk of indiscipline, others of a more understanding nature accepted that the crews were only releasing a terrible never talked about tension. For the next operation might well be their last. As, for so very many it was.

Notes, Chapter 3

1. *The Hardest Victory,* Denis Richards p114
2. *Bomber Offensive,* Sir Arthur Harris p103
3. *Soldier at Bomber Command,* Charles Carrington p38
4. *RAF Bomber Command 1936-1968,* Chris Ashworth p56
5. *The Hardest Victory,* Denis Richards p107
6. *The Hardest Victory,* Denis Richards p107
7. *The RAF 1939-45 Vol 2,* Denis Richards &
   Hilary St G Saunders p289
8. *The Six-Year Offensive,* Ken Delve & Peter Jacobs p84
9. *Selected for Aircrew,* James Hampton p203
10. *Selected for Aircrew,* James Hampton p205 & 206
11. *The Bombers,* Norman Longmate p181

Chapter Four

'You must never underestimate the English. They are never more dangerous than when they seem to be at their last gasp'.

Bruce Lockhart

'AIR MARSHAL HARRIS SAW IT AS HIS FIRST TASK TO highlight and dramatise the capabilities of Bomber Command. He had to promote a renewed faith in the proposition that the bomber offensive if persisted in, might itself force a decision or at least reduce the need for land fighting to well below the intensity (and therefore the casualty rate) of the First World War'. [1]

The need to have a well-organised training programme, ensuring sufficient aircrew were available for an expanding bomber force, was recognised. For obvious reasons the facilities for such a programme were limited and could not be successfully carried out in the U.K. Therefore an Empire Training Scheme, for pilots, navigators and bomb-aimers, was organised in South Africa, Rhodesia and Canada together with the Pensacola Scheme in the United States. Conditions in these countries ensured that flying programmes could proceed without possible interruption by enemy action or delays caused by inclement weather.

The expansion of Bomber Command was an urgent priority as was the equally urgent need to ensure that when more aircraft and newly trained crews did arrive they were not drawn off to support the Army in the Middle East, nor, on the navy's insistence drafted to Coastal Command. The latter caused Harris considerable concern for quite a period. Eventually he wrote to Portal pointing out with some bitterness that he was expected to supply everyone, whilst at the same time he was also expected to build his own force. 'Portal's reply was prompt. On 13th May he wrote telling Harris that Coastal and Army Co-operation had been informed that they could no longer draw on Bomber Command for trained crews and must, in future, provide from their own resources'. [2]

Whilst he was assessing the overall position of his Command, raids still continued. Kiel and Wilmhelmshaven were hit and mining operations carried out off the north west German coast, followed by a most successful raid on the Renault works at Billencourt near Paris, with 40 per cent of the buildings destroyed and production of lorries halted for many weeks. Unfortunately French civilians casualties were heavy despite the accuracy of the attack. On the 17th April 1942, 12 Lancasters flew by day to attack the diesel engine works at Augsburg. Only 5 aircraft returned once again underlining the fact that raids by daylight without a protective fighter escort would result in heavy losses in both aircraft and crews. And regrettably, the raid had little effect on the production of U boat engines.

It is not necessary to list chronologically the raids carried out by Bomber Command for they are amply recorded in books named in the Bibliography. Certain raids however, must be mentioned for they were landmarks in the increasing efficiency of the Command as a force to be reckoned with, brought about either by the introduction of new navigational aids or new tactics. For example, 'To test the incendiary concept Harris chose Lubeck as the target. There were two good reasons for this choice: it was easy to find, being a coastal town, and many of its buildings were made of wood and therefore a good target for incendiaries'. [3] 'The attack was carried out at very low level, many aircraft as low as 2,000 ft, it lasted 140 minutes'. [4]

'Daylight photographic reconnaissance revealed 200 acres

of built up area in the island city had been completely destroyed including 1,500 houses, the Town Hall and municipal buildings, the gas works, the electricity works and tram depot. South-west of the island, in the suburb of St. Lorenz, 65 acres of built-up area had been completely destroyed. North-east of the island, in the suburb of Marli, a 4,000lb bomb had destroyed ten large houses and partially destroyed 45 others over an area of 5½ acres. The Drager works, which made oxygen apparatus for submarines and aircraft, had been obliterated as had numerous other industrial concerns.

'But the greatest devastation was in the old town and the docks. It was so extensive that no goods could be sent through the town or the port for more than three weeks and the effectiveness of the port was reduced for many months longer'.[5]

With the successful raid on Rostock, Harris commenced to put into practice the idea of bombing a target in the shortest time possible, thus saturating the defences and the fire fighting services and now considered the possibility of attacking a major city with one thousand aircraft. He felt it necessary to demonstrate once and for all that Bomber Command could and would make a major contribution to winning the war, if he was given the aircraft and the technical assistance for navigational aids, radar and personnel.

Such a raid, he knew, would be a huge morale booster and it would also stifle the demands of the Navy for more aircraft to be drafted to Coastal Command to bomb submarine bases, a rather futile activity with the type of bomb then available.

Against this Harris knew that he was risking not only his front line bomber force of some 400 aircraft, but his reserves of men and machines at the Operational Training Units (O.T.U's) and the Heavy Conversion Unit (H.C.U's). It was a plan with great risks, yet, being the sort of man that he was, a spectacular sortie was necessary to win both public support and increasing backing for his future plans from official sources.

On the night of 30/31st May, 1046 aircraft set out, target Cologne. 'Between 00.47 and 02.25 that morning 3,300 houses were destroyed, over 2,000 badly damaged, more than 7,000 partly damaged. 12,000 fires raged in the city, the water mains were breached, gas mains exploded, power cables were severed and the telephone system wrecked. 36 factories were completely destroyed 70 severely damaged and more than 200 others damaged. The docks and railway system were badly damaged and the train system dislocated for months'. [6]

Denis Richards wrote, 'Considering the scale of the attack surprisingly few of the inhabitants were killed — 469'.[7] The 'Thousand-Bomber raid on Cologne did more damage to that city than all the previous 70 or more raids put together'.[8] Two more 1,000 bomber raids were carried out, but did not have the same success. However, Harris did prove himself to be a great military Commander and showed that, 'Germany could be effectively attacked by a powerful bomber force'. [9]

According to the Bomber Command War Diaries, 'German records show 2,500 separate fires were started . . . 3,330 buildings were destroyed, 2,090 seriously damaged and 7,420 lightly damaged . . . 36 large factories suffered complete loss of production, 70 suffered, 50-80 per cent loss and 222 up to 50 per cent loss . . . The estimates of casualties in Cologne, are, unusually precise. Figures quoted for death vary between 469 and 486. The 469 figure comprises 411 civilians and 58 military casualties, mostly members of Flak units . . . 5,027 people were listed as injured and 45,132 as bombed out. It was estimated that from 135,000 to 150,000 of Cologne's population of nearly 700,000 fled the city after the raid'. [10] This led Albert Speer to report to Hitler, 'that another six raids like this and Germany would be finished.' When interviewed after the war he queried why Bomber Command did not carry out more such raids. He did not seem to appreciate that weather conditions frequently caused raids to be cancelled, nor the interruption to the training of crews at the O.T.U's that putting such a large force into any single attack involved at that time.

Of the two less successful 1,000 bomber raids that took place, Essen was badly affected by ground haze and Bremen was covered with cloud, causing bombing to be scattered. However because of the number of aircraft taking part on those raids, 'the first serious attempts at streaming and concentration to overwhelm the defences, and to reduce losses, as well as the ground organization'. [11] These tactics and the control of routes to and from targets became a regular feature of future raids.

Two major events took place in 1942; the first was the resolution of the long running debate between Harris and the Air Staff. For some time it had been felt that a Target Finding Force was not only desirable, but necessary if the Main Force was to be led by experienced crews who had received special training and equipment, and who would also give special study to the development of pathfinding techniques. Harris did not like the idea of an elite force, as both he and the Group Commanders felt it would mean Groups losing their best crews to the new organisation and would damage morale. So with his usual forcefulness he vigorously fought the project.

However after an interview with the Chief of Staff, Commander in Chief Harris agreed to set up the scheme and, in a manner typical of him, having fought for what he believed to be right, when he was overruled he immediately put all his efforts into making the scheme he had opposed a success. He arranged that the crews would have a distinguishing insignia, namely the Royal Air Force 'eagle', to be worn on the lapel breast pocket beneath any medal ribbons. He also fought for the right of special promotion to crews who joined the Pathfinder Force. On 11 August 1942

58

the Force (PFF) was formed. It flew its first operational raid on 18 August and at this stage was not in possession of any special equipment other than that used by the Main Force. 'It was not until 1943 when new radar raids and effective target indicating bombs became available, that important changes in Bomber Command's ability and accuracy began to occur'. [12] Eventually, the new force became more proficient under the dynamic leadership of its chief, Group Captain (later Air Vice-Marshal) D. C. T. Bennett.

The Pathfinder Force had three basic marking techniques, known as *Parramatta* and *Newhaven* for ground marking and *Wanganui* for sky-marking. There were, of course, variations of these, for example when Mosquito aircraft commenced the raid with Oboe marking — this was named *Musical Newhaven*.

After many experiments a general procedure was adopted. First 'Illuminators' lit up the target area with flares. These aircraft were accompanied by 'Supporters', crewed by men learning illumination procedures and techniques and whose presence confused the defences and diverted enemy fire whilst the Illuminators successfully completed their task.

Next came the 'Markers', whose job was to positively identify the correct Aiming Point before releasing the Target Indicators on which the aircraft of the Main Force would release their bombs. 'Backers-Up' were crews who kept the Aiming Point accurately marked throughout the duration of the raid.

Markers and Backers-Up who arrived over a target to find it obscured by dense cloud would mark the Aiming Point with a special Target Indicator called a 'Skymarker', a coloured flare which descended to earth very slowly to indicate the release point for bomb aimers.

Keeping to the times laid down at briefing was of vital importance, as tail-winds might involve PFF crews arriving at the target too early. This often meant that doglegs (turning across the following bomber stream) were necessary, not a healthy pastime. Eventually as raids became more sophisticated, a very experienced Squadron Commander acting as a 'Master Bomber' would arrive a few minutes before the commencement of the attack and his plane would circle the area for the duration of the raid.

His task was to assess the T.I's accurate marking of the Aiming Point before calling in the Main Force to commence bombing. Should bombing errors occur such as 'creep back' (bombs falling short of the Aiming Point) or, later, drifting smoke obscure it, he would radio instructions to Backers-Up to mark it again thereby ensuring that a correct Aiming Point was maintained throughout the whole of the raid. His final responsibility was to assess the result of the raid before returning to base.

One of that elite band of Master Bombers was W/Cmd A.G.S. Cousens, DSO. DFC. whose nickname was Pluto the Squadron Commander of 635 Squadron. Most Master Bombers were pilots, but 'Pluto' Cousens was the exception, for he sported the pre-war half wing with the big 'O'. After the outbreak of war, 'N' for Navigator and 'B' for Bomb-aimer replaced the original trade of 'O' for Observer. It was a boost to morale to hear over the air the odd cheery remark, interspersed with his instructions about marking, or bombing the target, such as, 'Come on down its warmer down here'. He was acting as a Master Bomber on the Laon raid on the 22 April 1944 when sadly his aircraft was shot down and he was killed.

The second event to occur in 1942 was the arrival in Britain of the United States 8th Air Force, later to be known as 'The Mighty Eighth'. The Americans were slow in building up their strength and, like the British before them, had many lessons to learn. After flying in the clear sunny skies of the United State, conditions were somewhat different in the often stormy or cloud-covered skies of Britain and the Continent.

No-one can deny the great courage displayed by the American crews. However, many in their High Command allied to spin-doctors on the U.S. home front continually tried to hold the high moral ground by insisting that the 8th only engaged in precision bombing. A statement which time would prove to be somewhat incorrect. A Swiss military historian, Lt.Col. E. Bauer wrote in his book, *The History of World War II*, that 'The American crews nevertheless greatly exaggerated the degree of precision they could obtain with their Norden Bombsight'. The often quoted remark that, using the Norden they could, 'put a bomb down a pickle-barrel', was only possible in perfect flying conditions, and they seldom existed at that time in Europe.

Flying at 25 to 30,000 ft, in the close formation necessary for their defence, with very heavy flak bursting all around them and fighters coming at them from all angles — especially head-on — the lead bombardier would be having the same problems to contend with as the rest of his bomber group. How could all the bomb-aimers press their bomb-tits at the same time? It would be clearly impossible. Group Captain Cheshire wrote in his book, *Bomber Pilot* that, 'a bomb from 10,000 feet takes 25 seconds to fall. In that time the aeroplane has moved a mile or so, depending on its speed'.

Bomber Command now had the Mark XIV bombsight. It was, 'a masterpiece of design and precision engineering. It was fully stabilised by means of gyroscopes so that it could be used even when the aircraft was not flying in a straight and level attitude. Every Bomber Command aircraft was fitted with its own bombsight and unlike the American daylight bomber, every Bomber Command aircraft aimed its bombs individually, sometimes taking more than one run over the target'. [13]

Despite these differences, with the now tried and tested tactics of the PFF to find and mark targets with their new T.I's by night and the U.S. 8th Army Air Force stepping up their daylight raids, round-the-clock bombing of the Reich was about to commence and prove the truth of President Roosevelt's remark, 'Hitler built a Fortress around Europe, but he forgot to put a roof on it'.

For the American 8th Air Force, the daylight raids to which they were committed certainly required courage. Once their bombers crossed the enemy coast, German fighters would be waiting to attack the formations as they steadily flew both to and from the target. Aircraft nearing the target would see the sky ahead filling with great puffs of exploding flak, which led to the famous line-shoot, 'Flak was so thick you could put the wheels down and taxi on it'. And on leaving the target, they then had the hard task of battling their way back to meet their own fighter escort. Eventually they did have the benefit of being accompanied by newly developed long-range fighters such as the Mustang, Lightning and Thunderbolt, ensuring improved odds for survival.

When the Bomber Command crews, who normally operated under the cover of darkness, undertook some daylight raids, they were quite astonished.

Indeed they found it an enlightening experience. For example, as they neared the target area the great mass of bombers which were dotted all over sky, making up the bomber stream, began to manoeuvre into a narrowing column which enabled them to begin the approach and so to make their individual bomb runs to release their deadly cargo. Usually there were aircraft passing over and under each other as they jostled for position on the bombing run. At the releasing point, to see a 4,000lb bomb the shape and size of two dustbins tumbling out of an overhead bomb bay accompanied by a salvo of bombs streaking past was rather sobering. Nor, as sometimes happened, was it a boost to morale to see a comrade's aircraft explode in mid-air or watch a bomber ablaze and with a wing blown off, twirl like a fiery sycamore seed as it tumbled earthward. Anxious eyes watched to see if any parachutes appeared — which, unfortunately, was highly unlikely under such circumstances. So began the round-the-clock bombing of Germany, enabling the Allied air forces to make an even greater contribution to the final victory.

On January 14th 1943, Churchill and Roosevelt met in newly liberated French North Africa and the Casablanca Conference began, its purpose being the creation of a joint war policy. Far-ranging discussions resulted in the decision that the invasion of Sicily would have to be delayed, that Allied forces could not be committed to a cross-Channel invasion of Fortress Europe until 1944 and to a reaffirmation of the allies' unalterable objective: the unconditional surrender of Germany and of Japan.

The bombing of Germany was then considered at length and a directive resulted. However, 'the directive was *not* a directive in fact but something even more important, a general statement of policy set down, by the high personages responsible in the last resort for the conduct of the war'. [14] In it, Roosevelt and Churchill agreed that the bombing of Germany both by day and by night, on a massive scale, should be intensified, not only to achieve the progressive dislocation and destruction of the German military and economic system, *but also to undermine the morale of the German people to a point where their capacity for armed resistance is fatally weakened.*

This directive gives the lie to the charges so often levelled against Field Commanders like Harris, that they followed their own agendas and did just what they liked.

On 21st January 1943 an instruction formulating the policy to be followed by the Allied Air forces was issued, headed 'Combined Chiefs of Staff — Directive for the Bomber Offensive from the United Kingdom' [15] which set the parameters for the destruction of the German infrastructure and prioritised the order and kind of targets to be attacked.

This was received by Harris on the 4th February 1943 and accorded closely to his own thinking. 'Air Marshal Harris had been head of Bomber Command for not quite a year. He was an airman of very special qualifications and well-fitted to occupy the position, alike by training and temperament. Behind him lay more than a quarter of a century of experience, much of it gained in operating heavy bombers in night conditions of both peace and war'. [16]

In late January, at the Admiralty's insistence, Harris was instructed to bomb the ports of Lorient, St. Nazaire, Brest and La Pallice, the main submarine bases on the Atlantic coast of France. He was, however, firmly of the opinion that it was a misuse of air power, which would be better-employed bombing German factories. The concrete covering submarine pens was so thick as to be impervious to the type of bombs available at the time. The view of the Air Staff was that bombing the submarine bases would have little or no effect, except the destruction of French towns.

But, as he was obliged to, Harris, as usual, carried out his orders although he disagreed with the policy. Bomber Command hit the targets by night and the U.S. 8th Air Force carried out attacks on the same targets by day. 'On the 4th May Admiral Donitz was able to tell his colleagues: 'The towns of St Nazaire and Lorient have been rubbed out as main submarine bases. No dog or cat is left in the towns. Nothing but the submarine shelters remains'. [17] To quote Harris, 'the mine-laying campaign has had considerably more effect, than the destruction of the Lorient and St. Nazaire, on U boats using the bases on the west coast of France'. [18]

The most important industrial area in Germany was the Ruhr and on 5/6th March 1943 there began what the Commander-in-Chief called the 'Battle of the Ruhr'. Hitherto the towns in the area had defeated the bomber crews either because of low cloud or industrial haze. However, with the new navigational aids of Oboe and H2S and the new target

THE VICKERS WELLINGTON
Medium Bomber

THE HANDLEY PAGE HALIFAX
Heavy Bomber

LOADING UP A LANCASTER

'BOMBING UP' A DE HAVILLAND MOSQUITO
With a 4,000lb 'Cookie'

indicators now carried by the Pathfinder aircraft, the picture changed. From early March until the end of July the Ruhr towns were attacked. 'Between 5th March and 12th July Bomber Command carried out 43 major attacks on Germany of which two thirds were against the Ruhr'. [19] The Command chose not to visit the Ruhr on every single night lest the Germans massively increase their defences around the towns.

Other important targets were hit during the period of the Ruhr battle. On the 16/17th May the Mohne dam was breached and the Ruhr Valley flooded by 617 Squadron in the famous Dambuster raid. This had shown the greatest skill and dedication of the crews taking part and helped to prove that Bomber Command was capable of attacking a target with precision. Events were soon also to show its full destructive ability.

On the 24th July the operation codenamed 'Gomorrah' saw the beginning of the destruction of Hamburg. Window, those thin metal strips which blinded the German radar defences were thrown out of aircraft ahead of the Main Force and on the 27th July the 'Battle of Hamburg' reached its climax. A great firestorm took place and some 6,200 acres of the city were gutted. In all there were four RAF attacks by night and two by the USAAF by day and 87 of our bombers were lost plus 5 US aircraft.

After these raids, Albert Speer wrote, 'If the air raids continue on the present scale, within three months we shall be relieved of a number of questions we are at present discussing . . . I informed Hitler that armament production was collapsing and threw in a further warning that a series of attacks of this sort, extended to six more major cities, would bring Germany's armaments production to a total halt'. [20] 'In terms of destruction the results were unprecedented in air warfare and not to be exceeded until the Anglo/American bombing of Dresden and the American bombing of Japan'. [21]

There had been rumours since December 1942 that the

Germans had plans for 'Vengeance' or terror weapons to attack England. In April 1943 reports were received of the trials of a rocket weapon (which proved to be the later designated V2) at an experimental station at an isolated spot on the Baltic coast named Peenemünde. Photographic reconnaissance in June had shown several large objects that appeared to be rockets. Other photographs disclosed large unfinished building work in Northern France.

The night of 17/18th August, Harris and his Command's precision bombing skills were required and on this occasion Peenemünde was the target. According to briefings it would be attacked every night until it was destroyed, 'The crews were told that this was a matter of such extreme importance, that if the operation failed in its object on the first night it would be repeated on the next night, and on all suitable nights thereafter, regardless of casualties and regardless of the fact that the enemy would obviously do everything possible to increase the defences of the place after the first attack. They were to bomb from 8,000 feet, much below the usual operational height'. [22]

'Forty bombers were shot down and thirty two damaged. But the lives were not wasted'. [23] The crews who survived that first operation did not have to return! The consensus of those who studied the raid seemed to agree that it delayed the firing of rockets on England at the crucial time of the final preparations for D-Day. A few days later U.S. Fortresses attacked the mysterious buildings in Northern France.

About the same time more information arrived concerning experiments being made for a pilotless aircraft. This was subsequently confirmed by a, 'sketch drawn by a courageous Dane who, walking on the shore of the island Bornholm, had come across the prototype of one of those machines lying on the sand'. [24] This was in fact the V1 flying bomb, commonly known in England as the 'Doodle Bug' or 'Buzz Bomb'.

A new body was set up under the codename 'Crossbow' to

co-ordinate information and to give direction for measures to deal with the bomb. A joint effort by the Allied Air Forces was made, heavy and light bombers plus low level attacks by fighters and fighter-bombers were made on the launching sights. 'By the end of May 1943, 103 sites out of 140 had been destroyed'. [25] The first flying bomb fell on England on the 13th June, followed by one on Cuckfield and one in the Bethnal Green area. So the indiscriminate attacks on London and Southern England were to build up. It was unnerving to say the least, to hear the drone of an engine in the sky slowly coming nearer, possibly to even see the object, then, without warning the engine would cut out, followed by silence while everyone within earshot anxiously tried to predict where the bomb would fall. Then came a loud explosion as the bomb hit the ground. 'The first V2 rocket finally arrived on London on 8th September 1944. Had the V2s been available to Hitler three or even two months earlier to coincide with the initial invasion operations and the launching of the V1 flying-bomb attacks on Southern England, their impact would have been more serious than it later proved to be. Even disregarding the fact that without the attack on Peenemünde V2s would have been falling on Britain's south-coast ports in the vital invasion period of July 1944, the loss of two months' production was a deadly blow to Hitler's intentions'. [26]

The V2 rocket, though in material terms more devastating than the V1, was much less of a terror weapon. Travelling at over the speed of sound, it arrived before the sound of its flight. If you heard it explode, you knew you were still alive and if you didn't your worries were over.

'So the contest continued until on 27th March 1945 the last rocket fell on Kynaston Road, Orpington. It was the 1,115 to hit the United Kingdom. The total casualties from the rockets were 2,855 killed and 6,286 seriously injured: those from flying bombs being 6,139 and 17,239 respectively'. [27] The terror weapons which Hitler had boasted would strike civilians day and night, destroying London and breaking the morale of the enemy were in fact too late to influence the outcome of the war.

'The USAAF, encouraged by the strong attacks on 'fringe' targets in France, began to send its unescorted bombers over Germany in January 1943 — and it was then the slaughter began. It was not until the arrival of the first long range P52 Mustang fighter units in Britain that the crucifixion of the 8th US Air Force over Germany ended'. [28] They were to learn that the Northern European weather was very different to that back home and despite the armour and fire power of the B17 Flying Fortress, that without proper fighter escort their losses would be unsustainable. 'On the 17th August 1943 a double mission of 376 Fortresses was despatched to Schweinfurt and Regensburg. In a tremendous air battle sixty American bombers were shot down, mostly by German fighters'. [29] 'The skies of Regensburg were reported to be clear while Schweinfurt was obscured by ten-tenths cloud. To the RAF bomber crews, that would have mattered little: using radar markings, they would have rained the bombs down just the same. Not so the Eighth: at that stage of the war, Pinetree's edict was that bombardiers must see their targets'.[30]

The Regensburg mission was successful and the delayed Schweinfurt raid, which should have been over their target simultaneously to split the enemy fighters, took place 3 hours later. 'The Eighth had lost more aircraft in a day than it had lost in its first six months of operations'. [31]

The USAAF then chose targets in France and on the North Sea German coast. On the 14th October they attacked Schweinfurt again but with equally damaging results to both aircraft and crews. 'Of the 291 bombers which set out sixty were shot down, 17 badly damaged and a further 121 sustained less damage. Thus from an original force of 291 aircraft no fewer than 198 had been damaged or destroyed'. [32]

68

However four months later Schweinfurt was bombed by day, then by night by Bomber Command. Round the clock bombing was at last a reality. More importantly; the USAAF could from now on be escorted by the best long-range fighter aircraft of the air war, the Mustang, the Thunderbolt and the twin-boomed Lightning.

The night of 15/16th September saw the first use of the 12,000lb 'Tallboy' bomb in a raid on the Dortmund-Ems Canal.

With the aid of Oboe and H2S that old enemy of the bomber crews — bad weather — was on the brink of being beaten and the Pathfinder Force was seeking out targets and leading the Bomber Stream to them with growing accuracy. The next major campaign undertaken by Bomber Command was to be called the 'Battle of Berlin'.

Harris had previously stated that the air war could bring about an end to the conflict much sooner and thereby save land forces from the terrible slaughter of the first World War. Some critics scoffed at the idea and many writers, particularly military authors since 1945, have used this to mock Harris by pointing out that he had said, 'that a fleet of 4,000 bombers could win the war'.

At no time did he have that number at his disposal and it was not until 1944 with the combined strengths of the US Eighth Air Force and Bomber Command that there was anything near that total operating over Germany. No doubt, if such a force had been available at the beginning of 1943 the war might well have been shortened by a year at least. The theory cannot be proved or disproved as far as the European War is concerned. But it was to be proved without doubt in the war with Japan.

Harris always fought his Command to the maximum, giving aid even when protesting about the demands of the Army and Navy. He felt that the use of strategic bombers tactically was not the purpose for which they were built; that respite was being given to the Nazi economy of which Albert Speer would take full advantage. Some critics also claim that Allied bombing did not prevent German increase in war production but they forget that an expendable forced-labour force from conquered countries was readily available, and always used without scruple. Some '7½ million foreign and prisoners of war were incorporated in the labour force'. [33] Moreover it was possible for Speer to diversify plants throughout Europe making them more difficult for Bomber Command to locate and destroy.

With the onset of winter and the longer nights, Harris began to consider the bombing of Berlin, not an easy target for the weather always seemed to have the last word. He had earlier mentioned that with the combined forces of the USAAF and Bomber Command he could wreck the city from end to end, thereby beating Germany into submission. But now, the Americans, still without adequate supplies of long range fighters told him that they could not, at that stage, undertake deep penetration raids on targets such as Berlin and, therefore, could not meet his request for co-operation.

The Bomber Command campaign labelled 'The Battle of Berlin' began on the night of 18/19th November and raids continued intermittently until March 1944, when strategic bombers were to be made ready for attacks on French targets in preparation for D-Day. 'Time and time again, the crews fought their way to the target to find it covered by impenetrable cloud'. [34] Weather was indeed a very big factor in the conduct of an operation so far into Germany. Often, due to bad weather conditions, raids were either cancelled or, made more difficult due to heavy cloud cover. The Germans were also very efficient in lighting dummy areas in the surrounding countryside, to confuse the bomber crews. Then there were the defences; the enemy had ample time in which to defend his capital city.

'Surprise was virtually impossible to achieve . . . The

German Night Fighter Force was at the very peak of its strength and efficiency, battle-tried and very experienced . . . The sprawling conurbation which represented Berlin often defied the heroic effort of the Pathfinders to mark clearly the objective whilst the massed heavy gun batteries and hundreds of searchlights produced a nightmare unequalled in the experience of the veterans — and they were few indeed'. [35]

Once again, post-war critics have said this battle was a waste of men and materials, which could have been better deployed elsewhere; yet it is beyond dispute that it forced Germany to divert increased production of those anti-aircraft guns which would have been so useful on the Eastern Front to Berlin's defences, and also shifted fighter squadrons from the Eastern Front to protect the Reich's capital.

During this same period, Bomber Command continued with a programme of mine- laying as well as attacking other major enemy cities. Two raids are mentioned here due to the very heavy losses. On the night of 19/20th February 1944 some 823 aircraft set out for Leipzig, 78 failed to return; cloud had completely covered the city, involving the use of Skymarkers as aiming points. The problem seems to have been that the winds were not as forecast and, as a consequence, aircraft reached the target too early and had to orbit waiting for the Pathfinders to open the attack.

The other target was Nuremberg in which, again, badly forecast winds played a part, causing navigational difficulties. On the night of 30/31st March 1944, 795 aircraft set out, 'The first fighters appeared just before the bombers reached the Belgian border and a fierce battle in the moonlight lasted for the next hour. 82 bombers were lost on the outward journey and near the target . . . 95 bombers were lost in all . . . It was the biggest Bomber Command loss of the war'. [36]

Yet again weather had played a crucial role

'The bomber crews had been told at briefing that there would be high cloud along the route which could afford them concealment against night fighters. As the bomber crews flew across Belgium and German air space they realised the weather forecast was wrong: the skies were clear and they were fully exposed to the light of the half moon. They were also leaving dense condensation trails in their wake: although flying well below the height at which their tell-tale trails were usually produced. Another unforeseen hazard, was that due to unexpected high winds, the stream had already begun to lose concentration and to spread over a broad belt to the north of track . . . On reaching the target there was thick cloud'. [37] Although books have been written detailing the raids on the Ruhr, Peenemünde, Berlin, Nuremberg and Dresden, no one appears to have researched the Leipzig raid to date.

Even after the heavy bombers were switched both to other targets and the preparation for D-Day, the Mosquitos of the Light Night Striking Force of the Pathfinder Force which were capable of carrying a 4,000lb bomb, continued to make regular raids on Berlin. So regular were these raids during 1944/45 that some people nicknamed them, 'the Milk Run'.

'The operation on 24th March 1944 represented the last sixteen attacks on Berlin and the 35th in the overall campaign commencing 18th November. Of the 20,224 sorties dispatched 1,047 bombers failed to return with 1,682 damaged. The figures for Berlin alone are as follows: -

Total dispatched	9, 111
Missing	492
Damaged	954
Write off	95

It has been remarked that Berlin was a defeat for Bomber Command. This is not so, Sir Arthur's crews stood ready to return to the enemy's capital if so ordered: the nine per cent losses of 24th March were quickly made good and there was no lack of men, willing and eager to fill the gaps. It was

Nuremberg which called a halt'. [38]

There has been considerable controversy about the Nuremberg Operation not only by the historians but also by the various commanders involved i.e. Cochrane, Saundby and Bennett. Sir Arthur was probably more realistic than anyone when he stated that he was 'surprised that there were not more nights such as Nuremberg during the long campaign against Germany'. [39]

He now had to turn his attention to the forthcoming operation 'Overlord'.

Notes, Chapter Four

1. *Selected for Aircrew,* James Hampton p35
2. *Bomber Harris,* Dudley Saward p142
3. *The Six-Year Offensive,* Ken Delve & Peter Jacobs p91
4. *Uncommon Valour,* A.G. Goulding p57
5. *Bomber Harris,* Dudley Saward p125
6. *Uncommon Valour,* A.G. Goulding p63
7. *The Hardest Victory,* Denis Richards p131
8. *The Hardest Victory,* Denis Richards p131
9. *Uncommon Valour,* A.G. Goulding p65
10. *The Bomber Command War Diaries,* Martin Middlebrook
     & Chris Everitt p272
11. *The Six-Year Offensive,* Ken Delve & Peter Jacobs p99
12. *The Strategic Air Offensive Against Germany, Vol 1,*
     Webster & Frankland p434
13. *Selected for Aircrew,* James Hampton p202
14. *The RAF 1939-45 Vol 2,* Denis Richards

& Hilary St. G. Saunders p279

15. *Bomber Command,* Dudley Saward p186
16. *The RAF 1939-45 Vol 2,* Denis Richards
    & Hilary St. G. Saunders p280
17. *The Hardest Victory,* Denis Richards p164
18. *Bomber Offensive,* Sir Arthur Harris p139
19. *Uncommon Valour,* A.G. Goulding p86
20. *Inside The Third Reich,* Albert Speer p284
21. *The Hardest Victory,* Denis Richards p194
22. *Bomber Offensive,* Sir Arthur Harris p183
23. *The Bombers,* Norman Longmate p277
24. *The RAF 1939-45 Vol 3,* Hilary St. G. Saunders p145
25. *The RAF 1939-45 Vol 3,* Hilary St. G. Saunders p152
26. *The Hardest Victory,* Denis Richards p201
27. *The RAF 1939-45 Vol 3,* Hilary St. G. Saunders p175
28. *Before the Storm,* Robert Jackson p215 & 216
29. *Army Air Force in WW2 Vol 2,* p682-685
30. *Round the Clock,* Kaplan and Currie p67
31. *Round the Clock,* Kaplan and Currie p70
32. *The Strategic Air Offensive Against Germany Vol 2,*
    Webster & Frankland p39
33. *The Strategic Air Offensive Against Germany Vol 1,*
    Webster & Frankland p277
34. *Uncommon Valour,* A.G. Goulding p120
35. *The Bomber Battle for Berlin,* A/Cdr. John Searby p9-11
36. *Bomber Command War Diaries,* Martin Middlebrook
    & Chris Everitt p487
37. *Uncommon Valour,* A.G. Goulding p125
38. *Bomber Battle for Berlin,* A/Cdr. John Searby p157
39. *Uncommon Valour,* A.G. Goulding p129

Chapter Five

'In war, action provokes re-action, which in turn provokes further action and so on in a continuous process of sharpening the conflict towards extremes'.

von Clausewitz

SIR ARTHUR EXPRESSED HIS CONCERN WITH THE role allotted to Bomber Command when Overlord was being planned. Firstly because the strategic bomber force of both the RAF and the USAAF were to be under the control of General Eisenhower, the Supreme Commander of all the Allied forces. He wrote later: 'All such commitments in preparation for, or support of, the invasion had absolute and overriding priority. Thus the strategic bombing of Germany had lasted for almost exactly a year, and for no longer. This is a point which I cannot emphasise too strongly.

'The average man considering the effects of the bombing of German industrial towns is apt to think of it as a campaign, which went on for three years during which a force of 1,000 bombers regularly hammered away at all the enemy's main industrial centres. Actually only 45 per cent of Bomber Command's efforts during the whole of the war was directed against German cities and this 45 per cent included a number of exceptionally heavy raids carried out towards the end of war which were tactical rather than strategic in their aim and were designed to have a short term effect on the land campaign by blocking the communications of the Germany army'. [1]

He went on to say, 'I expected that the damage we had done to German industry — and for the size of the force it was most impressive — would be repaired in five or six months if we gave the enemy any respite from strategic bombing, and so I informed all concerned'. [2]

His second concern was that, 'The Allied bomber force had so far confined themselves entirely to strategic bombing and had never yet been successfully employed on a large scale in a tactical role. If they were to be used in this way, the USAAF had certainly been trained in precision bombing, and most tactical bombing is aimed at small targets, but without Bomber Command it was most unlikely that the Allies would be able to drop a large enough weight of bombs to have any decisive effect . . . all previous experience had gone to show the RAF's heavy bombers, with their futile ·303 defensive armament could not operate by day in the face of any serious opposition'. [3]

Martin Middlebrook sums it up simply, 'Despite his reservations about the new role, mainly over the ability of his force to hit the many small targets allocated to it without killing too many friendly civilians, Harris gave full and loyal support to the directions he received, both in the preparations for the invasion and in the support of the first weeks of the land battle'. [4]

Some historians have used the qualms he expressed as another example of his intractable nature, wanting his own way and wanting to carry on with his 'area' bombing campaign. In much the same way they continue to harp on about his remark that, give him '4,000 bombers and there would be no need to invade Europe'. It should be recalled that at the end of the war he still had only 1,400 heavy bombers at his disposal and that throughout his tenure as C-in-C, Bomber Command he was constantly emphasising the need for more aircraft.

Those same critics also seem to have overlooked the fact that during the early years of the war a lot of hard lessons had to be learned on the best way to win it and the learning was costly. Harris was possibly the only airman at that time who really understood what the role of the strategic bomber should be.

He had risen from flight commander in the First World War, through various posts to his present position. On the way he had instituted bomb aiming from the prone position, been instrumental in organising gun turrets for aircraft including the ·5 gun turret with which the later Lincoln bomber was armed.

He was not infallible and he did make some miscalculations. Those who repeatedly say he should have been relieved of his command, obviously have no conception of the pressures under which he constantly had to work and his enduring desire to save Allied lives particularly those of his own aircrews. Nevertheless he always accepted his orders and carried them out as did the Commander of the US 8th Air Force.

By March 1944, Harris had at his disposal some 65½ front line Squadrons with which he was now able to undertake the many tasks which he would be called upon to fulfil. In September 1939 Bomber Command had 23 front line Squadrons, so it had taken four and a half years to reach a credible fighting force. By April 1945 he still only had 98 Squadrons — significantly short of the 4,000 bombers he originally said would be required.

In the period prior to the invasion of Europe, Bomber Command not only played a crucial part in carrying out the, 'Transport Plan', attacking rail centres, railway services and repairing facilities in North West Europe, but also road and rail infrastructure. Furthermore it kept up the pressure on German Air power by attacking airfields in France.

'Though targets in France and Belgium bore the brunt of Bomber Command's pre-Overlord attacks, Harris also managed to operate farther afield. The always profitable mine laying continued — sometimes by more than 100 aircraft —

and Germany itself was not neglected'. [5] He was moreover delighted with the results of the accuracy of his crews and said, 'In fact I may as well say outright that Bomber Command's night bombing, from this point of view onwards, proved to be more accurate, much heavier in weight, and more concentrated than the American daylight attacks, a fact which was afterwards clearly recognised by SHAEF when the time came for the bombing of German troop concentrations within a mile or so from our own troops'. [6]

'On the night prior to the D-Day Landing Bomber Command made a significant contribution by not only attacking the coastal batteries, but flew diversionary squadrons not only to carry out jamming of enemy radar, but also to simulate invasion forces in the Pas de Calais area'. [7]

A 635 Pathfinder squadron air-gunner said, 'There was great excitement in the briefing room when the target was announced. When we got over the North Sea and near the French coast we ran into 10/10th cloud and my guns, the metal strips on the turret and the tips of propellers, were all tipped with the flickering blue sparks of St Elmo's Fire. Heading back to England in the early dawn, other Squadrons of planes passed us going the other way and, looking down, on the sea was a great armada of ships all heading for the coast of France; the long awaited invasion was at last under way'.

The calls to Bomber Command for assistance were frequent. From the Navy to bomb U-boat pens; from the Army to provide support for troops on the battlefields. In addition, with the first wave of Buzz Bombs being hurled against British towns and cities, launching sites became urgent targets. 'During the first week after the D-Day landings, Bomber Command flew nearly 2,700 operational sorties at night in support of landings, of which two-thirds were against road and rail communications . . . On June 14th Bomber Command was able to resume daylight raids, the first time for over a year. That such operations were now possible was due to the fact that the Main Force could be protected by Allied fighters for short penetration raids. The first raid involved over 200 Lancasters and was targeted against German naval forces off the Normandy beaches. Despite the protection of fighter escort, daylight operations still exposed the bombers to enemy fighter activity and, in poor weather and cloudy conditions, made accurate bombing difficult and increased the risk of French civilian casualties'. [8]

' . . . Le Havre and Boulogne . . . were attacked on June 14th-15th . . . At Le Havre very nearly every ship in dock, more than 60 all told, were sunk or damaged, and at Boulogne 28 vessels were sunk and many others damaged. In all some 130 naval and auxiliary craft were put out of action, virtually the whole of the enemy's light naval forces in the Channel area'. [9]

Bomber Command made two raids in support of the British and Canadian Army's breakout from the Normandy bridgehead. The first of these was the 21st Army's battle at Caen. Considerable criticism was aimed at the bombers who were accused of creating so many craters that the ground troops had the greatest difficulty moving forward through the rubble. However, Eisenhower on the 13th July 1944 wrote to Harris thanking him for his assistance (see appendix A). Then at the end of July the bombers supported a mainly American action and in August two further support raids took place, one being to assist the Canadians at the Falaise Gap.

Harris ensured that his Command assisted the invasion, even if putting a particular target out of action could result in heavy losses. Most of the major raids which involved such losses made the headlines at the time, or have subsequently been fully documented in many books. There were numerous raids that made a significant contribution, but earned no such headlines. Such were the raids on Revigny-sur-Ornain.

Oliver Clutton-Brock in the Preface to his book entitled, *Massacre over the Marne,* wrote, 'My curiosity was originally aroused when I noted that on three separate raids to Revigny in July 1944, a total of forty Lancasters were lost. But where was Revigny? And why was the target so important that three raids had to be mounted against it?' His research led to the discovery, 'that it was a small French town east of Paris'. And it was vital to the Germans because, although the town had no industry, the railway lines which passed through it were of great importance being continually committed to the rapid passage of troops and munitions. In consequence it was extremely strongly defended.

In explaining the horrendous Bomber Command losses, he also deals with, 'the 59 survivors from the 290 aircrew (of the 41 Lancasters), who found themselves alive on French soil'. And concludes 'The target should have been destroyed at the first attempt, but, as Sir Arthur Harris had promised Supreme Headquarters that it would be destroyed, RAF Bomber Command had to keep at it. Poor weather and the Luftwaffe saw to it that a heavy price was extorted'. [10] This raid is an illustration not only of the determination and dedication of aircrew to carry out their orders, but also of Harris to carry out his, to starve the German Army of vital requirements.

The 24th July saw the beginning of the Battle of Hamburg. Codenamed 'Gomorrah', Bomber Command attacked by night four times. Two attacks by day were made by the USAAF. Total losses were 87 Bomber Command bombers by night and 5 USAAF bombers by day.

After this series of raids, Albert Speer was extremely worried about the future for Germany if it was to suffer many more raids of that strength. And this raid surely gave the lie to the assertion that at this time in the war night raids were 'easier' than those made by day.

Events were now leading up to the raid which has caused considerable enduring controversy. Naturally, the media, which exists on controversy, first raising up idols and then

AIR CHIEF MARSHAL SIR ARTHUR HARRIS
C-in-C Bomber Command

BRIEFING AIRCREW FOR 'THE TARGET FOR TONIGHT'

A BOMBER STREAM

AIR VICE MARSHAL D.T.C. BENNETT
C-in-C Pathfinder Force

QUEEN ELIZABETH, THE QUEEN MOTHER
unveiling the statue of
Marshal of the Royal Air Force Sir Arthur Harris
before St Clement Danes in London's Strand

tearing them down, has always had a ghoulish interest in the raid on Dresden. Dresden had never once been visited by Bomber Command in the whole five years of the war. Wasn't it the home of Dresden China? What could be less warlike than that?

The railway lines which ran through Dresden were the terrible answer; these, and troops and supplies being pushed through the otherwise innocent town to hold back the advancing Soviet forces.

Stalin demanded action.

'The immediate, as opposed to the general, chain of events which brought about the Dresden raids began on 25 January 1945 when, to assist the Russian advance, the British Joint Intelligence Committee recommended air attacks on Berlin and other east German towns, and when Churchill enquired of Sir Archibald Sinclair, the Secretary of State for Air, what plans there were for — as Sinclair remembered the phrase — basting the Germans in their retreat from Breslau'.[11]

Sinclair's reply caused Churchill to react and demand further details on the morrow. 'With the Prime Minister obviously on the warpath, the events moved quickly. The same day Portal instructed Bottomley to seek approval of the Chief of Staff, SHAEF and General Spaatz for "one big attack on Berlin, Dresden, Leipzig, Chemnitz or any other cities where a severe blitz will not only cause confusion in the evacuation from the East but also hamper the movement of troops from the West"'. [12]

Max Hastings, not always seemingly to be a supporter of Bomber Command, or its Commander in Chief, wrote, 'It is ironic while Harris and Spaatz must accept much responsibility for continuing the area offensive after it ceased to have any strategic meaning, the Allied attack on Dresden cannot be laid at their door'. [13]

The Big Three, Churchill, Roosevelt and Stalin — met at Yalta 4th-11th February 1944 with their Chiefs of Staff. The

Russians requested help with the bombing of communications to prevent German reinforcements on the Eastern front. They mentioned Berlin and Leipzig and in fact, 'they clearly preferred to keep the RAF and the USAAF away from the territory they might soon be occupying. But the 'bomb-line' that was agreed with them placed the city of Dresden within the zone of Anglo-American air operations'. [14]

'After the orders of 27th January 1945 had arrived, Air Marshal Sir Robert Saundby, as Deputy C-in-C, first queried with Sir Arthur Harris and then, with the latter's agreement, telephoned Sir Norman Bottomley, who had signed it. Saundby was told the raid was to go ahead'. [15]

'At the conference, it was agreed that Portal's and Spaatz's bomber command should attack Dresden, the main centre of communication in the eastern area. Neither Harris nor Spaatz were happy with the order'. [16] 'The Official History (Vol. III pages 112-113) describes how Winston Churchill took a direct hand in the final planning of Operation Thunderclap — although Churchill tried to distance himself from the Dresden raid afterwards . . . So, Bomber Command was specifically requested by the Air Ministry, with Churchill's encouragement, to carry out heavy raids on Dresden, Chemnitz and Leipzig. The Americans were asked to help and agreed to do so'. [17]

'Unquestionably, the selection of these particular targets by the Joint Chiefs of Staff by three heads of government were fully justified by the military situation at that time. The choice lay between the preservation of Allied lives or German lives — and in the circumstances the decision had to be to preserve Allied lives at the expense of those of the enemy'. [18]

Again — 'Although Harris received his instructions to bomb Dresden, Leipzig and Chemnitz from Bottomley on the 27th January, he did not attack Dresden until the night of 13/14th February 1945 . . . Even then he sought, and received, from Bottomley by telephone that it was in order to attack'. [19]

From the records there is ample evidence to show that when Dresden was chosen as a target, it had been agreed that the 8th USAAF would make a daylight raid on 13th February and that Bomber Command would follow it up that night. In fact, bad weather prevented the US attack and it fell to Bomber Command to make the first raid and a two-pronged attack on the night of 13/14th February was organised. It was known that refugees fleeing from the Russian armies would swell the normal population and at the briefing of the crews of 635 Squadron (a Pathfinder Squadron in 8 Group) this was made plain. But it was emphasised that Dresden was an important communications centre for German reinforcement of the Eastern front, and that care must be taken when marking the aiming point, which was the railway station. These remarks were also addressed to the Backers Up. To the crews taking part it was just like any other raid except for the fact that Dresden was deep inside German territory and it would involve 8 or 9 hours in the air and under the constant threat of enemy attack for the round trip.

The raid was in two parts. The first was led by aircraft from 5 Group which opened the attack at 22.15 hours and the second wave arrived at 01.30 hours, led by the PFF of 8 Group. Ten and a half hours later, just after noon, on 14th February, '400 American Fortresses appeared over the city, though visibility was poor and their scattered bombing did little damage. Far more demoralising were the low level attacks of the escorting Mustangs, which, with no enemy fighters to engage, swept over the city machine-gunning anything that moved'. [20]

'Then again, on 15th February, they mounted another operation against the city with 211 bombers. The final raid of this series was made by the US Eighth Bomber Command on 2 March with 406 bombers . . . a further raid was made on the marshalling yards of Dresden on 17th April 1945, by 572 bombers of the US Eighth Bomber Command'. [21]

It should be stressed, 'that to Harris and the staff at Bomber Command who planned the attack, the Dresden operation was no different to scores of other heavy attacks mounted against Germany, except that high explosive bombs were in short supply at the time and more incendiaries were used. The Command's attacks had by now reached an extraordinary degree of technical efficiency; there was no possible way, however, that the staff at High Wycombe could anticipate the terrible fire storm which swept through Dresden causing such great devastation and the thousands of deaths in the city'. [22]

The number of people reportedly killed in the raid has varied with almost every published account — most favouring upwardly massaged estimates based on the 135,000 quoted by David Irving in his book *The Destruction of Dresden,* first published in 1963. However, 'Mr Irving candidly admitted his error in 1966 in a letter dated 7th July 1966 to *The Times;* he then quoted a report of the Dresden area police chief, in whose authority he said there was no doubt, which gives figures of 25,000 dead, and 35,000 missing'. [23]

There were some who said — and many who still continue to say — that with the war nearly over it wasn't necessary to have carried out such an attack, or, that Dresden wasn't a military target and the raid was morally wrong. Who, apart from post-war commentators or chairborne 'experts', could begin to believe that? And is it true? Only a few weeks earlier the Germans, although fighting fiercely on two fronts, had mounted an offensive in the Ardennes that caught the Allies completely unawares. Because of fog ground-support aircraft were unable to function, but Bomber Command was able to answer the Allied call for assistance. With the weather even grounding the Eighth Air Force, Bomber Command still managed to go out and bomb rail centres in Germany near the front and 'On 26 December, as the German advance faltered, clearer weather allowed Bomber Command to intervene nearer the battlefield . . . All this, taken in conjunction with the work of the Eighth Air Force and the tactical air forces, was a most powerful factor in the German defeat'. [24] Nevertheless, the outcome of the Ardennes offensive was a closely run thing and there was no evidence at all to suggest that the conflict would soon be over. It was known that the Germans were working on a V3 rocket and advanced ME 262 jet fighters were appearing on the scene so to say that the Germans were a spent force in February 1945 belies the facts. Over 300 bombers were lost from 14 February to the end of the war.

An article by Brian James in a *Telegraph Magazine* stated, that POW John Noble was one of the very few Westerners to witness from ground level the 1945 bombing of Dresden. Brian James quotes Noble, 'the best surviving rail links from the Eastern front pass from that city . . . Down the road from our factory was Germany's biggest defence plant still working'. There were many other industries producing war material in Dresden, as John Price, a naturalised American who served in th Polish Forces during the war, pointed out in a cogent letter he wrote in January 1995. 'Revisionists will again claim that Dresden was not a military target . . .

As an economic centre, Dresden ranked 6th in importance in pre-war Germany. During the war, over 3,700 industrial plants of various sizes worked full-time in Dresden for the Nazi war machine. Among them were such industrial giants as the world-famous Zeiss Ikon AG (Optics and cameras). The Dresden Zeiss plant was, with the main plant in Jena, one of the principal centers for the production of field glasses for the German Army, of aiming sights for the Panzers and the German artillery, of bomb-sights for the Luftwaffe, and of periscopes for the U-Boats. Besides Zeiss there were other internationally known firms producing radio sets, teleprinters, photographic paper, and telecommunication equipment.

'In the weeks preceding the bombing of Feb.13, the importance of Dresden as a war-production center increased considerably in view of the loss in Jan. 1945 of Upper Silesia (an industrial center second only to the Ruhr) to the advancing Russians. The destruction of the Dresden war-production center in Feb. 1945 meant a significant reduction of the effectiveness of the German Armed Forces.

'In addition, Dresden was one of the key centers for the German postal and telegraphic system and a crucial east-west transit point with its 7 bridges and a huge railway junction. This was particularly important at the time of the Russian offensive of Jan. and Feb. 1945 . . . Contrary to revisionist claims, the war was not 'almost over' in Feb. 1945. Germany still controlled extensive territories and actually produced surprises even after the raid on Dresden, for example in Hungary and in Lower Silesia. The Western Allies had not yet crossed the Rhine at that time. The greatest German threat, however, was that of the 'war-winning weapons' with which the Germans threatened the Allies until the very end of the war. The Allies had to take this threat very seriously. They knew that the V1 and the V2 existed but did not know what the V3, V4, etc would look like. Besides, they knew that the Germans were working on the atomic bomb. The war had to be brought to an end as quickly as possible with all available means. To achieve this, the Allies had no choice'.

Dresden, or what remained of it, was finally taken on 8th May 1945 by the Red Army.

At a briefing of war correspondents on 16th February 1945, an Associated Press correspondent filed an emotive dispatch alleging that the Allied Air Chiefs had adopted a policy of terror bombing German population centres. This caused a furore in official circles both in the United Kingdom and the United States.

'General Marshal stated publicly in America that the

bombing of Dresden had been carried out at a specific request of the Russians. General Arnold cabled Spaatz, seeking to be informed of the distinction between morale bombing and regular attacks on transportation targets in urban areas. Spaatz replied, 'that he had not departed from the historic American policy on Europe, even in the case of Berlin', and Arnold expressed himself entirely satisfied with the explanation. This, of course, was another instance of hypocritical cant; its inclusion in the American History and its incessant repetition by American writers did much, however, to spare Spaatz, Eaker and Doolittle from the vilification heaped upon Sir Arthur Harris in postwar years'.[25]

A typical example of the aforesaid is in Wilbur H. Morrison's book, *Fortress Without a Roof* published in 1982, 'Arnold's Headquarters in Washington sent an immediate enquiry following the raid, "Does this represent a change from American policy of bombing selected industrial structures to one of bombing cities"? Spaatz wired back, emphatically denying any such change in Strategic Air policy'. [26] There can be little doubt that in the propaganda and PR field the Americans were streets ahead of the British. So was the enemy.

'The Germans unquestionably won the second battle of Dresden, the propaganda struggle. The first High Command communiqué of 14 February 1945, stated merely that 'last night the British directed their terror-raids at Dresden,' but the German overseas broadcast picked up by the BBC Monitoring Service, were more outspoken. On 15th February Arabian speaking listeners in the Middle East were told 'it is obvious that these heavy raids were directed against the millions of refugees', and the German telegraph service, providing overseas pressmen, claimed that Dresden factories mainly manufactured toothpaste and baby powder'. [27]

The Russians in later years used this, having their own style of misinformation to keep the episode alive. Our own media has not been backward, over the years either in using this particular raid as a means of pointing an accusing finger at Bomber Command. For example on 17th February 1985, Channel 4 ran a programme with a predictable twist on the bombing of Dresden. Since much of the continuing controversy of Bomber Command and its C-in-C is based on this particular raid, a separate chapter is devoted to the media's treatment of the myths and statistics published since the end of the war.

On the night of 14th February 1945 Bomber crews again took off to raid Chemnitz, and also Rositz, a small oil-refinery near Leipzig. Attacks took place during the rest of the month on oil-refineries. 2nd March 1945 saw the last attack by Bomber Command on Cologne and during the month further raids were made on oil targets. The first 22,000lb bomb — the Grand Slam bomb — was used to destroy the viaduct at Bielefeld. Raids continued on oil fields and the shipyards at Hamburg. The Command also assisted the Army by bombing Wessel and Paderborn where the Americans were attempting to complete the encirclement of the Ruhr.

Bombing Kiel on April 2nd, 'the pocket battleship *Admiral Scheer* was hit and capsized; the *Admiral Hipper* and *Emden* were badly damaged'. [28] The night of 14/15 April 'was the last raid of the war by a major Bomber Command force on a German city . . . (and on the 16th April, at Swinemünde) 'the effects of one near miss with a Tallboy tore a large hole in the bottom of the *Lützow* and she sank in shallow water at her moorings'. [29] 26th April until 7th May saw Bomber Command Lancasters flying to the Continent to bring home British prisoners of war and also in that period 'Operation Manna' was undertaken dropping food to the starving Dutch, in large pockets of Western Holland.

On the night of 2nd/3rd May, Kiel was again attacked, 'because it was feared that the Germans were assembling ships to transport troops to Norway to carry on the war there'. [30]   The 9th May 1945 saw the unconditional surrender of all German Armed Forces.

So after five and a half years, the European leg of WWII was finally over and the aircrews and ground staff of Bomber Command had faithfully carried out every order which they had received, no matter how impossible nor how horrendous some of them had seemed. The nation rejoiced. Then came a snap General Election and a new British Government which, to its everlasting shame, refused to grant a Campaign Medal to those who had done so much — given so much — to achieve a great victory: the men and the women of Bomber Command.

The Butcher's bill had been heavy, yet volunteers to replace lost crews were never in short supply and came forward readily to carry on the battle. Equally vital to victory had been groundcrew, the thousands who had worked ceaselessly on cold, windswept airfields through some of the worst winters of the decade. These received no recognition either. Not even a nod for their efforts in maintaining and servicing the aircraft in their care.

An injustice is an injustice. But, then, those who in wartime, risk life and limb for their country — this country — should know what to expect. Much rhetoric, but no substance.

When a war is drawing to a close, the rhetoric begins: promises that things will be different in future and help available for the returning service personnel. Comes the day that the conflict actually ends and the celebrations completed, promises take a backseat and economy is the buzzword passing round the corridors of power. The shiny-seated Mandarins start holding their meetings and drafting papers for cutbacks in the numbers of men and women in the Services by reducing international commitments and by taking out of commission as many planes and ships as possible, as quickly as possible, so that Establishments can, in today's vernacular, be down-sized. Invariably defence is always the first political target for cuts, thus enabling Government to divert resources to pet schemes, to strike blows in the class-war or to 'buy' voters.

It is the politicians of the day who declare wars, but it is left to the so-called common people to fight them. And always as the conflict proceeds, a brighter future is promised to the population in general and the Services in particular. This spirit of generosity in official circles soon disappears when victory arrives.

After WWII, the British Government thanked all those who served with a gratuity. A cash payment. Not large. Economical, one might call it. It certainly wouldn't break any bank, nor bring any returning serviceman or woman out in a cold sweat.

The British Dominions did better. And the United States better still when Congress passed the 'The G.I. Bill of Rights' which offered returned ex-service personnel a key to a whole new future.

Notes, Chapter Five

1. *Bomber Offensive,* Sir Arthur Harris p191
2. *Bomber Offensive,* Sir Arthur Harris p192
3. *Bomber Offensive,* Sir Arthur Harris p196
4. *The Bomber Command War Diaries,* Martin Middlebrook
       & Chris Everitt p489
5. *Hardest Victory, Denis Richards* p 229
6. *Bomber Offensive,* Sir Arthur Harris p203
7. *Bomber Harris,* Charles Messenger p166

8. *The Six-Year Offensive,* Delve & Jacobs p157

9. *Bomber Offensive,* Sir Arthur Harris p210

10. *Massacre over the Marne,* Oliver Clutton-Brock p15/16 & 31

11. *The Hardest Victory,* Denis Richards p270

12. *The Hardest Victory,* Denis Richards p270

13. *Bomber Command,* Max Hastings p411

14. *The Hardest Victory,* Denis Richards p270/1

15. *The Bombers,* Norman Longmate p333

16. *Fortress Without A Roof,* Wilbur H. Morrison p377

17. *The Bomber Command War Diaries,* Martin Middlebrook
        & Chris Everitt p663

18. *Bomber Harris,* Dudley Saward p288/9

19. *Bomber Harris,* Dudley Saward p289

20. *The Bombers,* Norman Longmate p338/9

21. *Bomber Harris,* Dudley Saward p289

22. *Uncommon Valour,* A.G. Goulding p119

23. *A time of Courage,* John Terraine p678

24. *The Hardest Victory,* Denis Richards p262

25. *Uncommon Valour,* A.G. Goulding p150

26. *Fortress Without a Roof,* Wilbur H. Morrison p378

27. *The Bombers,* Norman Longmate p341/2

28. *The Bomber Command War Diaries,* Martin Middlebrook
        & Chris Everitt p693

29. *The Bomber Command War Diaries,* Martin Middlebrook
        & Chris Everitt p695

30. *The Bomber Command War Diaries,* Martin Middlebrook
        & Chris Everitt p703

Chapter Six

'One cannot go to war with compassion, total war means total death'.

Leon Uris

THE PREVIOUS CHAPTER COVERED THE REAL reasons for the raid on Dresden and its execution. Now we can look at what has happened since. Over the years, the media has continuously stoked up controversy about the raid, often misrepresenting the facts to blame Harris wrongly for the decision to mount it, which was in fact made by others.

For example, on 27th September 1979, in the *Daily Express*. Peter Grosvenor reviewed Max Hastings' book *Bomber Command*. He wrote: 'No man was a greater hero to his beloved bomber boys than Sir Arthur "Bomber" Harris . . . (He) saw that they wanted for nothing on the ground in the way of beer and extra rations. And rightly so . . . But that was during the war. Afterwards, as people remembered the death of 50,000 at Dresden (scarcely a military target) and 42,000 in the Hamburg firestorm, there was a revulsion of feeling. For, as Max Hastings rightly points out in his masterly new study — *Bomber Command* (Michael Joseph £8.50) — there is a distinction between *incidental* deaths when going for military and industrial targets and the *deliberate* and indiscriminate destruction of civilian life which was the purpose of Harris's policy of area bombing, also endorsed by Churchill.

'By going for the residential areas, Harris often missed the industrial areas in the suburbs. In the winter of 1944, he defied a directive to go all out against oil targets that would have shortened the war by months, as the Germans themselves well knew. At this point he should have been sacked, says Max Hastings bluntly'.

Thus Peter Grosvenor damned Harris with faint praise before repeating the usual misinformation about the Dresden raid together with the inflated casualty figures (culled from and, to his credit, later corrected by David Irving). He then went on to deride Harris's view that, at that precise time in late 1944, his bombers could be better strategically employed than in the blitzing of heavily defended oil targets with commensurately heavy losses of bombers and crews.

This was a mistake, Grosvenor said, 'as the Germans themselves well knew'. But was it, and did they?

At the time, Albert Speer, Hitler's Armaments Minister certainly thought so, he told Hitler so, but then had to rapidly reverse his opinion. He said as much in an interview broadcast on BBC Radio 4 a full year-and-a-half *before* Peter Grosvenor's comment appeared in the *Daily Express*.

In the radio programme he voiced his belief that Sir Arthur's judgement, at the time, had been demonstrated to be more sound than his own. 'In my memorandum to Hitler', he declared 'I said then what historians are saying now: that had those attacks been on our oil, our forces in September 1944 would not have been able to move at all. But, in fact, this would not have been the case. We had quite a high stock of gasoline and, to my astonishment, this stock was sufficient to supply our tanks for the Ardennes offensive'.

Of course the programme was not entirely impartial, but naturally also dwelt on the 'inconclusive nature' of the bombers' Battle of Berlin and on the Bishop of Chichester's 'grave doubts' about area bombing, namely whether the results justified the cost in lives and resources.

Eight weeks later, on 12th June 1978, the BBC returned to the fray when it transmitted a TV programme also entitled *Bombers*, heading the billing in the *Radio Times* with the biblical quotation Harris had used at the very outset of the

Allied Air Offensive against Germany: 'They have sown the wind and they shall reap the whirlwind' (Hosea 8. v7).

The object of the programme was to show the great losses suffered by aircrews, compared with the effectiveness — or otherwise — of the bombing campaigns, with contributions from the survivors of RAF Lancaster 'V' Victor and the American B17 Fortress named *Memphis Belle*.

The publication of Martin Middlebrook's book *The Battle of Hamburg* was another opportunity for Peter Grosvenor — *Daily Express*, 25th Sep 1980 — to perpetuate misinformation about Bomber Command. For example, 'Yet soon after "Bomber" Harris launched his policy of Area Bombing, involving the deliberate destruction of residential areas and the indiscriminate slaughter of thousands of defenceless women and children.

'Almost as big as Dresden (50,000 dead) was the RAF raid on Hamburg in July, 1943, where 42,000 died in a terrible 'firestorm' raid . . .

'In fact, in hindsight, Bomber Command consumed more resources than it destroyed. Hamburg quickly got back to life; Factories re-opened; commerce resumed'.

Emotive language but not accurate. Regretfully, articles such as these only help to promote and perpetuate some of the myths connected with Bomber Command as led by Sir Arthur Harris. As we have already seen, he did not initiate the policy of Area Bombing, he inherited it from his predecessors. It was put forward first by Portal, C-in-C Bomber Command in September 1940 when he suggested bombing German industrial towns. When Portal was made Chief of Air Staff he directed his successor, Air Marshal Pierce, in October 1940 to include attacking the morale of the German people in the air offensive. Thus the Area Bombing policy was in force when Harris took over Bomber Command in February 1942.

Moreover, accurate pinpoint bombing attacks were impossible in the early stages of the war due to the lack of adequate navigational aids for target finding and target marking. However, even at that stage, raids were already slowly beginning to divert men and munitions from the Eastern Front to the defence of German cities and national morale. Peter Grosvenor repeats the incorrect figure of the Dresden death toll — 50,000 corpses — and like many other journalists omits to mention that Dresden had first been bombed by the USSAF in October 1944, again in January 1945 and on two further occasions in March 1945 after the RAF raid on the night of 13th February 1945.

The suggestion that Bomber Command consumed more resources than it destroyed can be argued to the contrary.

Sir Arthur Harris died on 5th April 1984. A. G. Goulding in his book entitled *Uncommon Valour*, notes that, 'Independent Television News opened its main programme with the words "The man who ordered the bombing of Dresden is dead". This sentence was repeated in the popular press the following day'. The media has continued to promote this theme whenever Dresden is mentioned.

On the 40th Anniversary of the Dresden raid, the media had a field day. The *Guardian*, 13th Feb 1985. greatly exaggerated the facts and figures, 'A total in excess of one million is very probable, which means the West's usual estimate of 130,000 or more dead, rather than the East German figure (only 35,000) has a strong plausibility. It is very likely that the three attacks in 14 hours, by around 1,400 British and American bombers, killed twice as many as the Hiroshima bomb, and possibly ten times as many as died in London in the Battle of Britain blitz of 1940-1. To that extent, too, Dresden was 'a success'. It seemed not to matter that the war was virtually over when it happened'.

The *Daily Telegraph* ran an editorial on 14th Feb 1985 'THE BOMBING OF DRESDEN' and then stated, 'according to Western estimates it cost 130,000 human lives . . . The children, women and male civilians of a city associated, not with rocketry but ceramics, were the unimaginable trophy of a single night's area bombing on 13/14th February 1945, by which time the war was won, and no utility could be spun from superfluous death'. Emotive, but misleading, statistics of casualties were quoted and, of course, with the usual comment that 'the war was won'. That remark is obviously based on hindsight, since, no war is won until it is over.

Such articles prompted a spate of letters. Air-Vice Marshal D.C.T. Bennett (the Pathfinder Chief) wrote in the *Daily Telegraph*, 20th Feb 1985, 'Today we witness the despicable spectacle of many ungrateful people in this country denouncing us for daring to save their lives and their freedom — for doing our duty. This denunciation is based on carefully prepared Communist propaganda from East Berlin, and the hatred campaign has been actually supported by the media here. It has been orchestrated more skilfully than anything seen since, and many people fall for it . . . The readiness for some people to believe the anti-British Communist 'brain washing' of the last few days shakes one's confidence in our fellow British subjects and the loyalty of some of our media'.

John Terraine (Royal United Institute Chesny Medallist, President Western Front Association) wrote in the *Daily Telegraph*, 22nd Feb 1985, 'Your critical leader on the Bombing of Dresden (Feb 14) states that this event 'according to Western estimates cost 130,000 lives'. This figure probably derives from Mr David Irving's book, *The Destruction of Dresden* (1963), in which he gave a best estimate of 135,000 (compared with 71,379 at Hiroshima). This naturally horrified many people, but I wonder how many of them also saw Mr Irving's correction in the *Times* on July 7th, 1966, where he quoted the Dresden area police chief's final report giving a death-roll of 25,000, with 35,000 'missing' (presumed dead). The total roughly matches that of the Hamburg firestorm, July 27/28th, 1943. In a war of ghastly statistics, Dresden's are neither the worst, nor, indeed, abnormal.

'The date of the Dresden bombing is criticised: Feb 13/14, 1945, "by which time" you say "the war was won." But it was not. Hitler was still breathing defiance: the German army was fighting hard (it inflicted 300,000 casualties on the Russians in the battle for Berlin alone).

'It had just shocked the Western allies with its Ardennes offensive: there were grave fears of protracted resistance in the "national redoubt" and "werewolf" guerrilla warfare by Nazi fanatics; V-weapons were still in operation; 50 "U2" boats were in British or home waters, including some Type XXI which, if produced earlier, might have reversed the outcome of the Battle of the Atlantic and that would have been an Allied disaster . . .

'You say that "area bombing, eternally associated with Sir Arthur Harris, was wrong militarily and morally." It is nice to be so certain, however, responsibility for area bombing in 1945 rested with the British and American governments advised by the Joint Chiefs of Staff, cordially supported by the bulk of public opinion in both countries. Sir Arthur Harris's responsibility came some distance down the line'.

A further controversy arose over a film entitled, *Fireraiser*, attacking Harris and the bombing policy. Max Hastings in the *Daily Telegraph*, 10th Feb 1988 described, 'This film is in other words more than anything a political tract'. The film was withdrawn by Lew Grade.

In the *Daily Telegraph* on 3rd March 1989, W. F. Deedes in his column *Commentary* raised the question of the BBC marking the 50th anniversary of the outbreak of war in September with a play about Sir Arthur Harris. He wrote, 'The anniversary is a gift to our modern iconoclasts. I doubt if we shall be persuaded that we actually lost the war; but we shall certainly be told that we did not deserve to win it. At this distance it should have been possible to ferret out a lot about the darker episodes of the war. But most efforts will be directed at rewriting chapters which up to now we have considered glorious; and these efforts will be intended to reverse our opinion of them. I lay odds, for example, on someone telling us that most of the figures published during the Battle of Britain were false; and that, in any case, Hitler had already decided for other reasons not to attempt an invasion of Britain. There will be much in that vein. The valiant hearts of half a century ago will be made by some to look dupes in 1989 . . .'

The play was to be screened on 3rd September 1989. An article in *7 Days* had the heading 'SHADOW OF THE BOMBERS Does TV drama distort recent history? Tonight's BBC play *Bomber Harris* is flawed, argues Max Hastings . . .' Having set out his criticisms, in his penultimate paragraph Hastings writes, 'Dresden was merely one among a host of similar raids, which proved — in Bomber Command's terms — unusually successful. The entire British high command, above all Churchill, shared responsibility for the entire operation. It was Harris's folly in openly declaring after the event his contempt for 'German brass bands and Dresden shepherdesses' that pinned blame upon him in the eyes of history'.

The *TV Times,* week of 22nd-28th September 1990, on the page headed *Dear Editor* published a letter from Mrs H. M. Stephen of Farnham, Surrey, under the heading WAR CRIMES, 'Your recent correspondent thinks that the throwing out of the War Crimes Bill by the House of Lords was a national disgrace. Few people realise that Germany could demand the extradition of the now aged British bomber crews who flattened the beautiful city of Dresden - killing innocent men, women and children. In war, crime is not confined to the enemy'.

This brought the following replies under the heading WAR OF WORDS. 'I must reply to the letter by Mrs M H Stephens in the *TV Times* concerning her views on war crimes. The bombing of German cities was necessary to the war effort.

Where would she be today, and thousands like her, if our airmen had refused to do so? To class them as war criminals is utter rubbish — Mrs J Wallis (ex-WAAF) Sunderland, Tyne and Wear'.

V. Thompson, Stockton-on-Tees, Cumberland, wrote: 'So, a lady from Farnham thinks that British airmen, who bombed Germany, should be classed as criminals and extradited to Germany! I know this country harbours more cranks, do-gooders and plain idiots than ever before, but never in my wildest dreams did I think I would hear an Englishwoman — I presume she's English — condemn men who, in order to make Britain safe for her, helped to bring to an end a war which nobody but Hitler ever wanted'.

This correspondence prompted Douglas Radcliffe, Secretary, Bomber Command Association to write to the Editor, *TV Times* dated 28th September 1990, 'To single out the attack on Dresden as a war crime is wrong. If the Royal Air Force could have launched a similar attack in 1939, millions — yes millions — of lives would have been saved. The Battle of Britain saved us from defeat, Bomber Command paved the way for victory, losing 56,000 airmen in the fight against the Nazis, giving Mrs Stephen the freedom to make uninformed comment and the *TV Times* the right and freedom to print it'.

An extract from a letter published in the *Sunday Times*, 20th January 1991, from a Mr G. Harrap. 'INTELLIGENCE REPORT: The bombing of Dresden, so often described as wanton destruction, might have a more rational explanation. Sir John Colville, Churchill's private secretary, stated in *The Fringes of Power*: "A principal reason for the Dresden raid was the intelligence report received from the Russians, that one or possibly two armoured divisions had arrived there from Italy on their way to reinforce the defence of the Eastern Front" '.

An Essex University student, appearing in an ITV programme in 1991 stated, 'The bombing of Dresden was a war crime with no military purpose. The reason Bomber Harris didn't get any awards as other leading military commanders was a punishment for his war crimes'.

To quote Douglas Radcliffe again, 'I receive many letters, and visits from students requiring information about Dresden because they are wanting to write a thesis on the subject. I tell them to study Peenemünde instead, because if that had not been attacked the Allies might well have been beaten. The Nazis were ahead on both rocketry and heavy water for the atom bomb'.

When the proposal was made that a statue should be erected to honour Sir Arthur Harris, with its cost being raised with the aid of the Bomber Command Association and the RAF Aircrew Association — the unveiling ceremony to be carried out by the Queen Mother outside the RAF Church, St Clement Danes in The Strand — the protests began.

Daily Telegraph, 1st October 1991, headline: DRESDEN PROTEST OVER 'BOMBER' STATUE. Herr Herbert Wagner, Lord Mayor of Dresden, said the memorial did not belong in the Europe of 1992. 'I do not wish to mitigate Germany's war guilt, but Harris's carpet bombing against civilians was not militarily justifiable'. He states that, 'on Sir Arthur's orders, Dresden, Würzburg and Pforzheim, bombed in the last months of the war, were turned into "skeleton cities", with the loss of 35,000 lives over two nights in Dresden, and 20,000 lives over several days in Pforzheim . . .'

Note the German figure of 35,000, whereas many of our own journalists still quote the far higher figure; also the error of two nights when, in fact, Bomber Command only bombed on one night. 'Carpet Bombing' is an American term which was widely used to describe bombing during the Vietnam War; and there is no truth at all in the statement that it was a deliberate policy to 'bomb civilians'.

Simon Jenkins wrote an article in *The Times* entitled: BAN AIRBORNE TERRORISM. It commences, 'One good thing that might come out of the Dresden commemoration is the abolition of the bomb that destroyed it . . . But the obscenity of the free-fall bomb remains unchecked.

'What those too young to remember have found most shocking about Dresden is that the intention was to kill civilians. There was no pretence about this. The word 'terrorism' occurs again and again in the documentation, both before and after the event, not least by Churchill and the American commanders who actually authorised it, and were to create a firestorm. As in the ghoulish phosphorus raids on other cities, the intention was to burn, suffocate and fry civilians.

'For reasons that wholly elude me, bombs from the sky enjoy a moral protection not possessed by a soldier, despite the far greater danger experienced by the latter . . . February 14th is the anniversary not only of Dresden, but of the 1942 Air Staff directive that made Dresden possible. It focused bombing not on military targets, but "on the morale of the enemy civilian population".

'Harris's obsession with killing civilians emerges from his writings as maniacal. He disregarded the pleas of Allied commanders for bombing of the retreating German supply-lines. He left oil deposits untouched, and as a result permitted the German Ardennes offensive. Speer, in his memoirs, was incredulous of this waste of bomber resources. History shows that Harris's insubordination prolonged rather than shortened the war. He was out of control. He was, as Churchill sensed, a fanatic.

'An entire theory of conflict — that aerial bombardment of civilians can alter political decisions by war commanders — was put to the test in the cause of inter-service rivalry. No attempt was made to prove its validity . . .'

Today's moralists who argue with hindsight seem to forget

we did not start the war; that the road to all-out aerial bombardment was started by the Nazis, commencing with Guernica followed by Warsaw, Rotterdam, London, Hull, Liverpool, Birmingham, Coventry and Belgrade, to name but a few of such targets.

Air Marshal Sir Harry Burton, Chairman of the Memorial Fund, wrote: *Daily Telegraph*, 6th May 1992, 'In the light of all the comment about the Bomber Command Association's intention to erect a statue of Marshal of the Royal Air Force Sir Arthur Harris, may I put the bombing campaign in perspective. First, it was the policy of the British and American government's, supported by the vast majority of the British people, to destroy German industry and its supportive infrastructure, most of which was based in and around cities . . . It was tragic that the main aim involved the destruction of cities, but the German government could have prevented that by surrendering, or at least minimised casualties by evacuating women and children, as we did when our cities were attacked early in the war . . . I would draw attention to the views of Albert Speer . . . when he said, "In my opinion the bombing campaign was the greatest lost battle on the German side"'.

Squadron Leader P Tomlinson wrote: *Daily Telegraph*, 27th May 1992, 'As the pilot and personal assistant to Sir Arthur "Bomber" Harris during the first two years of the war . . . I taped his version of events. He said, "I got the orders to bomb Dresden from the Supreme Allied Commander, General Eisenhower. I checked with Air Ministry and they confirmed that it was to be bombed. It was bombed and thereafter they all turned their backs on it . . . Albert Speer, Hitler's minister, admitted after his release from Spandau, that without the bombing of Germany the war could have gone on endlessly, and certainly the Allied invasion could never have advanced from Normandy to central Germany in 11 months".'

The unveiling of the statue of Harris enabled all and sundry to express their views in the media, and no opportunity was lost to take full advantage. On the 31st May 1992, Queen Elizabeth, the Queen Mother, graciously addressed the assembly before unveiling the statue, and was interrupted several times by groups of protesters which, the press said, included pacifists, the Peace Pledge Union and members of the Revolutionary Communist Party. Most of those arrested were less than 25 years of age and were not even born during the war. On 1st June the media covered the unveiling fully with reports and photographs and it could have been hoped that this would see the end of all the controversy. But . . .

In April 1993 the BBC ran a programme in the *Timewatch* series entitled *Battle of the Bombers* which included a studio discussion that dealt mainly with Britain's bombing policy in WWII. This resulted in a letter from a gentleman named Tom Baistow appearing in the *Daily Telegraph*, 10th April 1993 under the heading *Bombing: Other side of the coin.*

'Sir — The BBC Timewatch programme *Battle of the Bombers,* shown last Wednesday, failed lamentably in its presumed task of putting into historical perspective the most controversial campaign of the Second World War for the millions who were either children or unborn at the time.

'For one thing, the programme signally omitted to establish the wider context essential to any understanding of Britain's decision to opt for and continue strategic bombing: namely the introduction of terror bombing by the Luftwaffe. First practised at Guernica during the Spanish Civil War, there followed the destruction of Warsaw and Rotterdam and the indiscriminate blitzing of Coventry, London and other British cities; then, after the invasion of Russia, the flattening of Soviet towns as the German army advanced.

'Although the German contributors were given generous camera time to remind us of the dreadful fate of Dresden, there were no civilian survivors of the British blitz to explain what it was like to see women and children die here — long before Dresden's people faced the same horror. Nor, in a studio full of RAF, Luftwaffe and academic participants, was there one British ex-soldier to add a dimension to the discussion on the effects of carpet bombing on the morale of Allied troops fighting their way across Europe.

'May I, as someone who served in an armoured brigade from D-Day onwards, point out that BBC broadcast accounts of RAF raids, which we listened to on our tank radios, were a significant morale booster, not least for men who had lost, and were continuing to lose, relatives and friends in the cynically indiscriminate rocket and flying-bomb attacks on London.

'Every "Bomber" Harris mass raid got a rousing cheer. One supposes that the civilians in our war factories were no less heartened by what we regarded, in the desperation of those fearful days, as "good news".

'Further, I believe that whatever the armchair pundits may assert, the raids considerably helped to soften Reichswehr resistance . . . The rights and wrongs of mass bombing can never be assessed in terms of statistics alone'.

In the *Sunday Telegraph*, 18th April 1993 there appeared the following comment, 'Why does the BBC feel obliged to put out so many programmes unfairly critical of Britain's war record? The recent *Timewatch* on Dresden was a particularly bad example of this habit. Surely there are enough newspapers and commercial TV stations willing if not eager to denigrate this country without the BBC having any need to get into this less than edifying act'.

A highly controversial film, *Death by Moonlight*, was shown on August 7th 1994, on Channel 4 in the series, *The Valour and the Horror*. The CBC in Canada originally broadcast it, twice in 1992. It was written and produced by two Canadian brothers. The broadcasting of this film raised considerable anger, both in Canada and in Britain.

Paul Hensher in the *Daily Telegraph* of 8th August 1994 concluded his criticism by saying, 'but on the whole this was a serious subject, treated with every flippancy of the worst TV documentary clichés'.

Denis Richards, a respected historian, wrote: *Daily Telegraph*, 9th August 1994, 'While pleased that your television critic rightly condemned the Canadian programme *Death By Moonlight* as "serious subject treated with every flippancy of the worst documentary clichés" (review Aug 8), I would like to add that it has also been criticised by Canada's Senate as "a seriously flawed assessment". I was commissioned to produce a report for the Canadian Broadcasting Corporation's ombudsman on the programme in the light of the row in Canada, I'm astonished that Channel 4 could spend money on such a shoddy and erroneous production . . . As a result, I'm afraid that the Right of Reply programme which Channel 4 is planning to show on Saturday is no substitute for the good the company could have done had it decided simply to say "no thank you" to the film's producers'.

W F Deedes wrote a piece in *Notebook* in the *Daily Telegraph*, 15th August 1994 entitled *History becomes an editorial*. He concluded his article by saying, 'I think the episode illustrates how far down the road of "film editorials" about past events we in this country have gone. Our own film directors are more sophisticated than Brian McKenna. They have learned how to assemble a version of history which, however wide of the mark, attracts little public criticism. We simply swallow it. So, alas, do our young'.

So great was the reaction that Channel 4 had to broadcast a special edition of *Right to Reply*. This necessitated the recalling of staff from holiday to enable them to put out a programme in which Air Marshal Sir Ivor Broom was given the opportunity to challenge the inaccuracies and misrepresentation expressed in the Canadian film. At the end of the programme a man in the studio audience stood up and said that he was a Canadian and on behalf of his countrymen he would like to apologise.

In the *Toronto Star* in September 1994, Kenneth McDonald — vice-chairman of the Bomber Harris Trust — wrote an article, stating, 'Former Canadian aircrews were angered particularly by the film's denigration of their wartime role by the second episode of *Death by Moonlight*: *Bomber Command*, and they formed the Bomber Harris Trust to sue the CBC and others for defamation . . . Brian McKenna, who produced the series, has his own preconceived idea of the bomber offensive that in the words of Hitler's armaments minister Albert Speer, "opened a second front long before the invasion of Europe . . . This was the greatest lost battle on the German side".

'In McKenna's view, Canadian bomber crews were badly led by Air Marshal Sir Arthur Harris, whose portrayal by an actor in the film was unrecognisable to all who knew him, yet McKenna was quoted as saying of the caricature that if he were "remaking the film now, I guess what I'd have to say is that I'd make it stronger".

'This is the source of the controversy: McKenna makes assertions to fit his preconceived view of the bomber offensive and then was obliged to falsify facts to support his assertions . . . British ITV's Channel 4 exposed British viewers to McKenna's denigration on Aug 7. By mid-afternoon of the next day Channel 4 reported 174 telephone calls, of which all but two condemned its errors and tone. In the *Daily Mail*, historian Andrew Roberts, who saw a pre-screening, called it, "a grossly insulting distortion of the truth. It would be a disgrace were Channel 4 to screen it without first removing some of the monstrous inaccuracies it contains . . . Hitler's propaganda chief Dr. (Josef) Goebbels could not have done a better job".

'John Turnbull, the Bomber Harris Trust's honorary

registrar, who appeared on Channel 4's Right to Reply programme after the showing, spoke for his comrades, living and dead, when he said: "As a Canadian, I would convey an apology to our British colleagues, and to Britons generally, for the fact that a Canadian produced a film of this nature'".

As a result of the constant misleading information pumped out by the media, the RAF Bomber Command Association decided to produce a documentary film which would tell the full story of Bomber Command for the first time: The first video entitled "Reaping the Whirlwind" became available at the RAF Museum's shop at the end of 1997 and a second video has followed.

In the *Sunday Times*, 22nd January 1995, Norman Macrea wrote an article under a banner headed, OPINION, entitled, *Salute the men who bombed Dresden*. He commenced by saying, 'We approach one of 1995's most grisly 50th anniversaries . . . Apologies for that horror are being insultingly organised by bishops then too young, and other "caring people" then unborn, to understand what actually happened . . . Nazi propaganda shouted 250,000 civilians died that night. Some of today's apologists to Germany still say 100,000. The most careful German historian, with new access to East German files, says fewer than 25,000'.

In the *Sunday Times*, 29th January 1995, Patricia Clough under the banner NOW DRESDEN'S HORROR IS RECALLED wrote, 'About 20,000 were recorded dead or fatally injured. Today it is estimated that another 10,000 died among the ruins, bringing the total to about 35,000. But for years, first the Nazi's, then the Communists, claimed a death toll many times higher'.

So, with the passing years, columnists seem at last to be recording more accurate figures.

Professor Frank Musgrove (ex 149 Sqdn. RAF, Beverly, East Yorkshire) in the same newspaper wrote a letter in which he said, 'As the navigator of a Lancaster bomber who took part in the raid, I had no doubt at the time, and have none since, of the military importance of the mission. At a briefing of my Squadron in Norfolk we were told that a build-up of German soldiers and armaments in Dresden was a serious threat to the Russian advance and the raid was necessary solely to help Russia. My only doubt about the enterprise now is not that we destroyed a German city (and the troops and armour) but that we facilitated a Russian advance deeper into the heart of Europe than otherwise may have been the case'.

In *Centre Point* in *The Spectator*, 4th February 1995, Simon Jenkins wrote, 'Harris was a fanatical believer in bombing cities. He was contemptuous of the oil targeting strategy. Like many commanders scenting victory, he was not interested in helping the army and longed to see his bombers carry the vanguard of victory over a flattened wilderness. Many Germans, including Speer, later wrote that one of the things that could have ended the war in 1944 (and saved several hundred from the gas chambers) would have been the re-direction of Allied bombing from cities to oil supplies . . . Harris's insubordination was the central catastrophe of the last war . . The Dresden raid was part of the destructive frenzy by an insubordinate commander, unleashed by Churchill to bring a gift to Stalin at Yalta'.

In the *Daily Telegraph*, 11th February 1995 under the heading, NOT RIGHT, BUT NOT EVIL, Max Hastings stated in the course of his article, 'Knowledge of the cost of British lives, industrial effort and the prestige of senior airmen made the RAF resistant to growing evidence that "area" attack was far less effective than they had hoped in crippling German industry, while American attacks on oil plants were yielding impressive results . . . Portal (Chief of Air Staff) was close to exasperation with the obsessive determination of Sir Arthur Harris, C-in-C of Bomber Command, to complete the destruction of German cities. Portal was convinced of the case for joining the American precision attack. Yet he did not dare to sack Harris'. This of course is an opinion, certainly not fact, as Harris did offer his resignation to Portal, suggesting he should find a new C-in-C. Portal, however, didn't think January 1945 was the time to make such a move and urged Harris to stay and do as much as he possibly could towards the oil campaign.

In an official biography, *Portal of Hungerford*, Denis Richards writes of Portal, 'As when he commanded a squadron, he remained in Whitehall a disciplinarian. If he gave an order he expected it to be carried out, regardless of difficulties. He also expected staff to use their initiative'. [1]

In the *Daily Telegraph*, letters to the Editor, 12th February 1995, Martin Middlebrook wrote, 'It would be a pity if Dresden and its firestorm were to be remembered as just another RAF area bombing raid . . . This was part of a widespread "Operation Thunderclap" with attacks on other German cities designed to cause a massive collapse of German resistance against the current Russian offensive'. In the same block of letters, Brian Pennington wrote, 'No one in their right mind would seek to glorify war. None the less, it is ironic that it was a survivor of Dresden, Dr Manfred Scholz, who was left to acknowledge (on the BBC's 6 o'clock news) the logic of the RAF's actions in the bombing of that city, while apologists from Britain sought to make scapegoats of our servicemen who were pursuing what their superiors considered a way to bring the war to an early close'.

In the *Spectator* 18th February 1995, the following letter from Guy Hartcup appeared under the heading BOMBS AWAY. 'Simon Jenkins's argument (*Centre Point*, 4th February) that the British owe the Germans an apology over the bombing of Dresden is vitiated by a mismatch of historical inaccuracy, prejudice and hindsight, and does the aircrews of Bomber Command, who risked their lives night after night flying to targets in Germany, a grave disservice.

'First, the misapprehension about the C-in-C Bomber Command, Sir Arthur Harris: he was a Field Commander and as such took his orders from the Chief of Air Staff, Sir Charles Portal. He never initiated bombing policy. While disagreeing, often in blunt letters, to Portal regarding the bombing of precision targets like oil and the support of the armies in Normandy, in the end he always complied. He was too much the regular officer to be the autocrat that popular legend would have us believe.

'Second, the background to the Dresden raid: although in January 1945 the western allies had repulsed the Ardennes offensive, the Wehrmacht appeared far from defeated; no one knew whether Hitler had another V weapon or even an atomic weapon up his sleeve. The Red Army was advancing on Germany and Eisenhower, as Supreme Commander in the West, asked that the strategic bombers should support the Russians. For that reason four cities which were important communication centres in the line of the Russian advance were chosen for attack (Operation Thunderclap). Dresden was selected as a target because it had not been heavily attacked before. Indeed, Harris initially opposed the attack as the target lay deep in Germany and the bombers had to cross belts of anti-aircraft defences. Moreover, the Command had recently suffered heavy losses in raids on Berlin.

'On the night Dresden was attacked weather conditions were good and the German defences negligible; hence the success of the raid. On the following day the city was pounded by the heavy bombers of the Eighth U.S. Air Force, but the target might well have been Leipzig or Chemnitz.

'There was indeed a revulsion against area bombing after Dresden. After the war aircrew of Bomber Command, unfairly, were not awarded a campaign medal although they alone had carried the war to the enemy while the land forces were being built up after Dunkirk. For those, however, who had suffered the Blitz and V weapons there was, at that time, little sympathy for the people of Dresden'.

The *Sunday Telegraph* on 19th February 1995 published an article entitled, *Why I flattened Dresden*, by Harris. It is based on a letter addressed to Norman Bottomley dated the 29th March 1945. The full text was published by Max Hastings in his book, *Bomber Command*. The following extracts set out some of the views held by of Arthur Harris on the bombing campaign and the charges made on the policies he carried out. Marked PERSONAL & TOP SECRET it commences:-

'Dear Norman

It is difficult to answer indictments of which the terms are not fully revealed and for this reason I cannot deal as thoroughly as I should like . . .

To suggest that we have bombed German cities "simply for the sake of increasing the terror though under other pretexts" and to speak of our offensive as including "mere acts of terror and wanton destruction" is an insult both to the bombing policy of the Air Ministry and to the manner in which that policy has been executed by Bomber Command. This sort of thing if it deserves an answer will certainly receive none from me, after three years of implementing official policy . . .

Dresden was recommended by the Targets Committee as a transportation target as well as on other grounds . . . I have always held and still maintain that my Directive, which you quote, "the progressive destruction and dislocation of the German military, industrial and economic systems" could be carried out not only by the elimination of German industrial cities and not merely by attacks on individual factories however important these might be in themselves. This view was also officially confirmed by the Air Ministry . . . and is now enabling Allied soldiers to advance into the heart of Germany with negligible casualties. Hence the only question which I have to answer is this; would "confining ourselves to

111

more precise concentration upon military objectives such as oil and communications behind the immediate battle zone" tend to shorten the war more than persistence in attacking cities?

'We have by no means always a free choice in this matter. Weather conditions frequently constrain me to decide between attacking cities and not attacking at all. When this happens it is surely evident that it is expedient to attack the cities.

'We have never gone in for terror bombing and the attacks which we have made in accordance with my Directive have in fact produced the strategic consequences for which they were designed and from which the Armies now profit . . . Attacks on cities like any other act of war are intolerable unless they are strategically justified. But they are strategically justified in so far as they tend to shorten the war and so preserve the lives of Allied soldiers.

'H.E. is seriously limited in supply. Incendiaries are not. All these factors must therefore also be considered, and the inevitable answer is that either we continue as in the past or we largely stand down altogether. The last alternative would certainly be welcome. I take little delight in the work and none whatever in risking my crews avoidably . . .
Yours ever,
Bert
Air Marshal Sir Norman Bottomley, KCB, CIE, DSO, AFC
Air Ministry, Whitehall SW1'.

This letter surely shows that "Bomber" Harris like many of his contemporaries who had served in WW1, including 'Monty' (who was often accused of being too cautious) were always conscious of the many hundreds of thousands who were killed and maimed on the battlefields of France in that War. He was determined to avoid a repetition, the Allied Armies certainly moved rapidly once they crossed the Rhine and the casualties were comparatively light.

Peter Paterson in his *Review* in the *Daily Mail,* 11th September 1996 said, 'Last nights film *Bomber Command; Reaping the Whirlwind* was probably as close as we shall get to an apology by Channel Four for the disgraceful Canadian-made documentary they screened two years ago on the same subject. Television companies hate to admit error so, as well as making amends to the many viewers who were outraged by the depiction of the RAF''s wartime bomber crews as war criminals in *Death by Moonlight-Bomber Command;* Channel Four defiantly showed it again after the screening of *Reaping the Whirlwind.* It was, however, shamefacedly tucked away in a late-night spot after most of us would have been tucked up in bed'.

The Times on 6th November 1996 recorded that the 'Official Record of Bomber Command is published at last'. In the article which followed Michael Evans, Defence Correspondent, states 'Not a word of regret appears. The commander in chief wrote in his *Dispatch on War Operations* that the heavy bomber did more than any other single weapon to win the war'. He goes on to say, 'Herr Boog, recently retired as service director of research at the German Armed Forces Military History Office, goes out of his way to acquit Sir Arthur of the charge of war crimes'.

The publication referred to is most interesting, Sebastian Cox in the Editorial preface to Sir Arthur T Harris's *Dispatch on War Operations* says, 'Harris has become indelibly associated with two events: the destruction of Dresden in February 1945 (the only conventional bombing raid of the Second World War), and the policy of area bombing itself. Neither is an entirely accurate reflection of Harris's responsibility. To a large degree he has become the scapegoat for policies approved and, in the early years, designed by others'. [2]

In December 1997, in a programme broadcast by the BBC, a professor in response to a statement from a member of the studio audience that 'they (Bomber Command) bombed the civilians of Hamburg and Dresden', noted that this was, once again, a distortion of the truth. He went on: 'In all the abuse levelled at Harris and Bomber Command over the Dresden raid it seems to be forgotten that the USAAF also played its part in the attack on the city'. [3]

Gordon Musgrove said, 'The Americans had already attacked the Dresden marshalling yards on January 16 before the proposals had been put forward . . . It is curious, too, how often after the war the Germans who needed American financial aid, played down the USAAF's in the attacks'. [4]

Surely the time has come to lay to rest, for all time, the charge that in what happened to Dresden 'the responsibility rested with Sir Arthur', He was, after all, only passing on to his crews the unequivocal orders which he had received from others.

Notes, Chapter Six

1. *Portal of Hungerford,* Denis Richards p177
2. *Sir Arthur T. Harris, Dispatch on War Operations,*
        Sebastion Cox, Editorial preface
3. *Uncommon Valour,* A.G. Goulding p157
4. *Pathfinder Force,* Gordon Musgrove p171

Chapter Seven

'The will to conquer is the first condition of victory'.

Unknown

The C.V. of Arthur T. Harris, born 13th April 1892

Bugler, 1st Rhodesian Regiment, October 1914. When it was disbanded he sailed to England.

Joined Royal Flying Corp, October 1915. Qualified for his wings June 1916. Went to France and saw service with 11 and 19 Squadrons.

Returned to England; became Flight Commander 329 Squadron, Northolt, charged with defence against Zeppelins.

Promoted to Major 1918. After the war, granted a permanent commission in the RAF as Squadron Leader.

Posted to India in 1921 to command 31 Squadron.

Transferred to Iraq (Mesopotamia) 1922 to command 45 Squadron; where the tribes were described by him as, 'truculent and warlike'. It was during his service there that he developed night flying tactics, and where 'by sawing a hole in the nose of our troop carriers and making our own bomb racks we converted them into what were really the first long range heavy bombers'. [1] Also experimented with bombing from the prone position.

1924 returned to England and went to Army Senior Officers' School. Then posted to command 58 Squadron, Worthy Down. 'This was the first heavy bomber squadron to be reconstructed as such, after the war and the first to get back to night training for night operations'. [2]

1927 attended and completed Staff Course at Camberley, promoted to Wing Commander. From his own account the course did not impress him very much although he said, 'I had a great admiration for Montgomery (later Field Marshal), who was an instructor at the time: I had the greatest admiration for his precision of statement and lucidity as a lecturer and also for what I perceived, as an airman, his ability and breadth of view as a soldier'. [3]

Posted to Egypt as Senior Staff Officer at H.Q Middle East Command.   Returned to U.K to command Flying Boat Squadron at Carshalton.

Promoted Group Captain, July 1st 1933 and moved to Air Ministry, Directorate of Operations and Planning.

1934 made Deputy Director of Plans: appointed Director of Plans, 1935, becoming Air Staff member of Joint Planning sub-committee of the Chiefs of Staff Committee. It was while at the Air Ministry in 1935 that the specifications for the Manchester, Stirling and Halifax were laid.

1st July 1937 promoted Air Commodore.

1938 Air Officer Commanding No. 4 group in Yorkshire, before being sent on a purchasing mission to the USA.

July 1938, posted to Middle East as AOC Palestine and Jordan.

1st July 1939, promoted Air Vice-Marshal.

September 1939 became AOC No. 5 Group, in Lincolnshire. It was there that the Hampden bomber began the mine-laying campaign. 'This was the beginning of a highly successful campaign forcing the enemy to divert more and more of his war effort to anti-mine laying devices, and ship building for replacements and repairs, and before the end of the war, drove him to engage 40 per cent of his naval personnel in minesweeping; it also put an immense strain on the enemy's alternative communications'. [4] It was also during this period that he arranged for the gun mountings in his bombers to be re-designed so that 'it doubled the effective fire-power and eliminated the blind spot'. He went on to say that it was the same firm, Alfred Rose & Sons at Gainsborough who designed and 'made the ·5 gun turrets, when official channels had let us down completely and spent much of their energy protesting that nothing could be done while we got on and did it'. [5]

In 1940 Portal, who at that time was Chief of Staff Bomber Command, was appointed Chief of Air Staff and he sent for Harris to ask him to be his Deputy Chief of Staff. It was there that he acquired his reputation for putting junior officers in their place and tackling 'serious over manning'.

June 1941, promoted to Air Marshal. He then headed a delegation to the USA, where he met many influential people, some of whom he would work with back in the UK later in the war. It was during this period that Portal offered Harris the post of Air Officer Commander-in-Chief, Bomber Command.

This, then, is the background of the man who, only a few weeks from his 50th birthday, took over this vital post at the end of February 1942. 'He was a man expertly qualified to direct the operations of this important command'. [6]

In April 1942, the future looked very bleak. America had been shocked by the events at Pearl Harbour, and although she had declared war on Germany, it would take time before her vast resources could be geared to full capacity and many months before she could build her forces in the UK. From every quarter of the globe, bad news seemed to be rolling in. In the Far East the Japanese had overwhelmed Hong Kong, Malaya and Singapore, and were on the borders of India. Both HMS *Prince of Wales* and HMS *Repulse* had been sunk by the Japanese air force.

British forces lost Greece and Crete in rapid succession and the Royal Navy lost command of the Mediterranean. Italian frogmen sank two battleships in Alexandria Harbour; *Ark Royal* was attacked and sunk by U-boats and Malta was under siege by the Luftwaffe.

To complete the global picture Leningrad was besieged, the German army was on the outskirts of Moscow and soon to over-run the Caucasus oil fields. The Battle of the Atlantic was in full flood and U-boats sinking increasing tonnages of Allied shipping, carrying urgently needed supplies to British ports. The Royal Navy, used to fighting against heavy odds, was just about holding its own. And the Americans also had their own setbacks in the Pacific, losing many Islands to the Japanese who could now come within bombing range of the Northern Territory of Australia.

And in North Africa in June 1942, Rommel had made a sudden attack, sending the British and Commonwealth troops back through Libya, until almost all the land gained in earlier battles was lost.

There was little chance that the necessary build-up of forces to invade Europe would be possible in the foreseeable future, despite the pressure from Stalin and Communist inspired demonstrations in Trafalgar Square, for 'A Second Front Now!' The Allies fortunes in that period were, to say the least, at a low ebb. However, Harris was sure that he had the answer: he would start on a Second Front by taking the war to the German homeland. In fact his command was the only one that was in a position to actually take the war to the enemy at that time.

Anyone who writes about Bomber Command invariably discusses Harris and his manner in carrying out his duties. A common theme runs through many of them, as the following extracts will show. Max Hastings, in describing Harris, said he, 'had something of the earthy, swaggering ruthlessness of an Elizabethan buccaneer. A broad man of medium height, his piercing eye gave him immediate presence in any company. "There are a lot of people who say that bombing cannot win the war", he declared to a newsreel interviewer a few weeks after taking over at High Wycombe, in the crisp, clipped tones that cowed so many havering staff officers. "My reply to that is that it has never been tried yet. We shall see." He gave no sign of fearing God or man and, in Washington, his outbursts of frankness had left behind a trail of savaged American military sensitivities'. [7]

That statement concerning Americans is directly contradicted by Dudley Saward (who wrote *The Authorised Biography "Bomber" Harris*). 'Harris spent eight months in America and established the RAF Delegation in Washington on efficient lines, quickly providing it with immensely influential contacts . . . Harris, immediately on his arrival, established contact with Roosevelt and Harry Hopkins, and with Averell Harriman, General Marshall, General Arnold and Robert Lovett . . . A few days before Harris returned to the UK a newspaper commented 'Heading homeward to England in the next few days will be Air Marshal Arthur T. Harris and Mrs. Harris who have made a record number of friends since they came here last year . . . They had, indeed;

119

friends who were to be of the utmost importance to Britain in the struggle that lay ahead. Harris had in eight months paved the way to the incredibly close co-operation that developed between Britain and US Forces as the war progressed in Europe . . . General Arnold expressed his appreciation dated 4th February. It read:

'My Dear Harris,

Upon the eve of your departure from the United States, I desire to express my appreciation and that of the United States Army Air Forces for your splendid co-operation and ever present spirit of helpfulness.

Your presence here aided materially in bringing our airplanes up to a combat standard and also in changing our organisation from one of peacetime training to one of preparation for war.

In the name of the Army Air Forces I wish you God speed and good luck.

Very sincerely yours,

H. H. Arnold

Lieutenant-General,

Chief of the Army Air Forces, USA' [8]

Describing Harris, Max Hastings is quoted again. 'His dry cutting, often vulgar, wit was legendary throughout the RAF, as was his hatred of the British Army and the Royal Navy'. [9] It is not surprising that he had little liking for his sister services. His experiences with the Army in India in earlier years and, during the inter-war years, the frequent attempts by both the Army and the Admiralty to divide up the Air Force and, later, Bomber Command, 'was under threat of extinction, not from the enemy but from the Admiralty, the Army and those politicians who had no faith in a strategic bomber offensive . . He was determined to infuse a new confidence in the Command: and it is a measure of this remarkable man's force of personality that within a few days of his taking over as Commander-in-Chief, somehow, every one in the Command was convinced that this was the turning point'. [10]

Healthwise, Harris suffered from ulcers, smoked heavily and drank in moderation. Most seem to agree that he was a born fighter for what he believed in and did not suffer fools gladly. 'In red tape and for those who were slaves to it, he had absolutely no time whatsoever'. [11] The C-in-C was no prima donna like Montgomery or 'Blood and Guts' General Patton. He seemed to shun personal publicity, and journalists were treated no more indulgently. He refused press conferences and this may explain why the RAF has not always had the best coverage in the media.

The letters and memoranda that passed between Harris and Air Ministry were often strongly worded. Perhaps, as it has been suggested on occasions he overstated his case, but, having forcefully made his point, when he was over-ruled he devoted all his single-mindedness to carry out his orders. A classic example is the founding of the Pathfinder Force. He and several of his group commanders, felt it would be wrong to create an elite force, which would also have the effect of taking the best crews from the Squadrons. When he was over-ruled, not only did he institute a promotion scale, but decided on the emblem (the Skyhawk) which PFF crew-members would wear on the flap of their tunic pockets.

When the plans were being made for the invasion, he made known his views that giving the enemy respite from strategic bombing would permit damage to be repaired in a short period of time. Nevertheless he recognised that, 'there was no alternative if the most formidable military problem of this and possibly any war was to be solved and Europe was to be invaded across the sea'. [12]

He would put pen to paper and write things in the heat of the moment without thought as to the adverse effect they might have on others; 'it was a major reason why he was so unpopular among some of his fellow commanders. Furthermore, it illustrates something of his scepticism towards the other two fighting services, which made relations between Bomber Command and them continually difficult'. [13] 'Unable to suffer patiently the foolish or the inefficient Harris had at the same time a quick sense of humour. He was sparing of speech, yet inspired the deep respect of his subordinates. Publicity he disliked, and he went to great trouble to evade it'. [14]

'Frequently, his ideas and actions ran counter to those held by the Air Staff in Whitehall — but there are precedents — Harris abhorred place seekers, bureaucrats and 'yes men' who wished to placate an enemy so vile as were the Nazis. Alas, he fell victim to the Stracheys and the Attlees — the bishops and others'. [15]

Much has been made of correspondence exchanged between him and Portal. Often stating his views and possibly overstating his case when he felt strongly, but because of his close relationship with his superior, he felt he could express himself so openly. That he did not always have a high regard for the other services is no doubt a result of his experiences with the Army in India and his time at the Staff College at Camberley. Regarding the Royal Navy, he seemed to feel that they were still fighting the last war, considering aeroplanes as artillery platforms; not wanting to accept that battleships were outdated and could be destroyed from the air.

Moreover, their constant insistence that the U-boat pens should be bombed was a mindless irritation at a time when, in fact, there was no bomb capable of penetrating the fifteen feet of reinforced concrete which sheltered them. Both services were guilty in his eyes of constant attempts to have Bomber Command broken up. He certainly needed to be an utterly determined, single-minded conviction airman.

There is an ill-informed idea of how Harris carried out his

duties, particularly when it came to deciding which targets were to be attacked. These decisions were, in many cases, dictated by the weather and the special requirements of Government and the other services. The impression seems to be, that he stalked into the Operations Room and, standing before a big wall map, stabbed his finger on a town and said, 'We'll bomb this tonight and the aiming point is Willi Schmidt's shop', and that he then went into purdah for the rest of the day. An obviously ludicrous picture!

A more likely scenario is that upon his entering the Operations Room his team of advisers would gather round and the first question to be settled would be how the weather was behaving over the Continent and, equally important, what would it be like over England hours later, when aircraft were due back at their bases. What was the phase of the moon; what force and direction the winds? Then the target list, drawn up by the Ministry for Economic Affairs and from what the Army and Navy wanted, had to be considered. A decision would finally be made and the target for that night would be named. Harris would then depart, leaving his subordinates to get down to the detailed planning of bombloads, petrol, routing, any diversionary raids, PFF marking strategy, aiming point over the target and the number of aircraft to be involved. All this then had to be passed down to the Group HQ's who in turn advised the Squadrons.

Subject to the weather, this was the grinding routine which had to be followed for almost every day of the war. Harris was to remark, 'For that matter I wonder if the frightful mental strain of commanding a large air force in war can ever be realised except by the very few who have experienced it. While a naval commander may at the most be required to conduct a major action once or twice in the whole course of the war, and an army commander is engaged in one battle say once in six months or, in exceptional circumstances, as often as once a month, the commander of a bomber force has to commit the whole of it every twenty-four hours; even on those occasions when the weather forces him to cancel a projected operation, he has to lay on the whole plan for committing the force. Every one of these operations is a major battle and, as much depends on the outcome, success is as vital and disaster as grave, as on any other occasion when the whole of a force engages the enemy . . . It is best to leave to the imagination what such a daily strain amounts to when continued over a period of years'. [16]

He was a remote figure from his squadrons, yet the bomber crews had a great respect and affection for him. It was quite common to hear remarks such as, "Butch" (short for Butcher) 'would have the "Mad Major" out with his chopper tonight', yet they still 'pressed on regardless'.

At Squadron level, the Battle Order would be posted on the notice board in the Sergeants' and Officers' Mess, listing the aircraft and the crews who would be taking part; time of briefing and pre-flight meal times. Preparations then involved the air-testing of aircraft after which, on landing, crews returned to their respective Mess or billet, dependant upon the time of briefing. The latter usually took place in a long wooden pre-fabricated hut on the airfield. The first thing crew members' eyes looked to, as they entered the hut, was the very large wall map at the far end. This map of Europe displayed the 'operational route', a red tape threading its way — with any necessary changes of heading — from the home base to the target destination. The homeward journey was, of course, by a different route. After the briefing the aircrew had their pre-flight meal of bacon and eggs, after which they made their way to the locker rooms to don their flying gear. Preparations completed, it was time to board the waiting crew bus or lorry to be taken to the respective aircraft dispersal point.

Time to take off: the crews climbed aboard, the pilots

124

started up the engines, and in no time the airfield would reverberate with the noise of aircraft engines being run up. The planes taxied onto the perimeter track, lined up behind each other and lumbered their way to the runway where the Controller's caravan was parked. When the green light flashed from the Aldis lamp, operated by the Airfield Controller, the lead plane would turn onto the flare path. The pilot opened up the four Merlin engines, unlocked the brakes, and thundered down the runway finally rising into the air, to be followed one by one by the rest of the squadron. Harris's 'old lags', as he was later to call them, were on their way to the target for that night.

The return flight home had its own problems; apart from possible serious damage to the aeroplane and shortage of fuel. There was always the possibility of wounded on-board, weather closing in earlier than expected and/or the added hazard of fog.

Weather conditions played a crucial role when decisions were made about the operations for the coming night, especially in the winter months. At Downham Market, two Pathfinder squadrons (No's 635 Lancasters and 608 Mosquitos) were fortunate in being stationed at one of the few airfields which had the system known as FIDO. (Fog Intensive Dispersal Operation).

This consisted of long pipelines in which holes, pointing skyward, were placed on either side of the main runway. When operational, they burned vaporised petrol, the heat from which was intense but virtually smokeless, warming the air and lifting the fog, to give a clear view just above the runway. The effect of the rising air on the landing bomber would be a tendency to float above the runway and a reluctance to touch down on *terra firma*. Flying home across the North Sea, FIDO when lit, showed as a reddish glow in the distant sky, giving the impression that an enemy air-raid was in progress.

After the war, the first Bomber Command re-union was held at the Royal Albert Hall. It was packed. Various leading figures were present; Vera Lynn had been invited to attend and to sing during the evening. The proceedings opened with a telegram from the Queen being read out, followed by several speeches from the platform. The assembly then began to get restive and started to shout ever louder and louder 'We want "Butch"' over and over again. Finally the opening speaker came forward and held up his hand gesturing for silence; when the hall was quiet he said, that 'Sir Arthur Harris regrets that he is unable to be with you tonight as he was on his way to South Africa'. He then proceeded to read a telegram received from him. When he finished, loud cheers and whistles erupted it from the audience.

Over the years there have been many Bomber Command re-union dinners. One of the most memorable was organised by two air-gunners, Ray Callow and Harry Pitcher, at the Grosvenor Hotel, Park Lane, London on 30th April, 1977, in honour of Sir Arthur's 85th birthday. It was attended by 750 veterans and their wives. At the conclusion of the meal, Sir Arthur made an outstanding speech, which was an assessment of Bomber Command from his own personal recollections and records. (see Appendix B). It was received with a standing ovation and loud cheers from the gathering.

After the formal part of the evening was completed and the guests had departed upstairs, the author, following later, observed that a queue was forming outside a curtained room. Ever curious, he too stood in line and when he passed through the curtain, there at the head of the queue was the guest of honour, the legendary figure himself; short, thick set, perhaps a little rotund, shaking hands as the guests came up to him.

It was a memorable moment not only to meet, but to actually grasp, shake and feel the cool, firm grip of a man who had so frequently been charged as being, 'a remote figure from his squadrons', yet whose leadership had so inspired Bomber

Command. His wife Lady Harris was standing by his side, begging people not to engage him in conversation as he was losing his voice. He continued to attend these annual dinners every April until his death in 1984, yet none surpassed that occasion.

Notes, Chapter Seven

1. *Bomber Harris,* Sir Arthur Harris p22
2. *Bomber Harris,* Sir Arthur Harris p23
3. *Bomber Harris,* Sir Arthur Harris p24
4. *Bomber Harris,* Sir Arthur Harris p39
5. *Bomber Harris,* Sir Arthur Harris p40
6. *Through the Bombsight,* Andrew Maitland p176
7. *Bomber Command,* Max Hastings p158/159
8. *Bomber Harris,* Dudley Saward p100/101, 105/106
9. *Bomber Command,* Max Hastings p159
10. *Uncommon Valour,* A.G. Goulding p55
11. *The Great Ingratitude,* James Fyfe p91
12. *Bomber Offensive,* Sir Arthur Harris p192
13. *Bomber Harris,* Charles Messenger p65
14. *Daily Telegraph* – 7 April 1984, A/Cdr G.S. Cooper,
        Air correspondent
15. *Everlasting Arms,* A/Cdr John Searby p190
16. *Bomber Offensive,* Sir Arthur Harris p72

Chapter Eight

'Action will remove the doubt that theory cannot solve'.

Unknown

COMPARISONS ARE OFTEN DRAWN BETWEEN THE methods and results of Bomber Command and the US Army Eighth Air Force. Those same sources usually question the Allied bombing campaign, especially the part played by Sir Arthur Harris. Unfortunately, because of their easy access to the media they readily have their views published. 'As the years since D-Day and victory have passed there arose the desire on the part of historians; sensation writers, some journalists and television writers and producers to assassinate the character of Harris'. [1] This view is shared by Chaz Bowyer, 'In very recent years it has become almost fashionable to denigrate the policies and actions of the Allied bombing offensive against Germany in particular, with fellow moralists broadly denouncing specific examples of overtly destructive raids *et al* . . . Too many of them harp on about how many German civilians, especially women and children, were killed by our bombs, and set out to condemn Bert Harris and other top brass for so-called area bombing policies. These so-called experts all forget — or just don't understand — that this country was engaged in a total war against Hitler and his regime. And total war meant that every man, woman and child was part of their country's war effort'. [2]

'The main implications of strategic bombing have been the subject of heated and prolonged discussion for a half a century or more . . . The net result, at the end of years of argument is that practically nothing has been resolved . . . The simple truth is that once the first shell has been fired and the first bomb dropped, once the nations are irrevocably committed to a course of total war, the words 'morally' or 'immorality' have little meaning. In total war, there is no dividing line between the two; there are only varying degrees of harm. When two nations are more or less evenly matched victory invariably hinges on the ability of one antagonist to punch harder and faster, with all the means at his disposal than his opponent. And in such a conflict, there are no civilians'. [3]

Simon Jenkins is ever ready to moralise when expressing his views on matters relating to anything connected with bombing; for example, 'The war was all but over and military installations around Dresden were not targeted. The attack was a modern version of the medieval 'putting a city to fire and the sword' . . . The only centres church and palaces packed with refugees were targeted, rather than railway or barracks on the outskirts . . . saying sorry costs nothing'. [4] Very emotive, but it misrepresents the facts and why are apologies required? Did we start the war? Those wishing to justify their arguments against strategic bombing always trot out morality.

'In all the abuse hurled at Harris and Bomber Command over the Dresden attack it seems to have been forgotten that the USAAF also played its part in the attack on the city. The vast American fire-raising attacks on Japan by General Curtis Lemay's B29 Super Fortresses, in which 84,000 people were killed in one day, have also escaped censure. These attacks, with their dreadful casualties, were carried out before an atomic bomb had been heard of'. [5] In fact the Americans bombed Dresden three times after the RAF raid.

In a perfect world there would be no wars; it would be outlawed, The United Nations would not only have International Laws, with an International Police Force to enforce such laws, but demand full co-operation from the International Community. As Pascal said, "Law without force is impotent." Unfortunately national self-interest still governs international affairs. At UN Assemblies there have been many recent examples.

When faced with what was known of the actions of the Nazis before the outbreak of war, the subsequent actions after war was declared and, what has come to light since the unconditional surrender, there can be no doubt the greater immorality would have been to let Germany's industries and its transport system spew out the weapons of war. In modern warfare, as has already been stated, every one is involved, not just those fighting at the front, but also those left behind to work in the factories, the transport infrastructure and so on. Whilst Bishop Bell — the leader of the churches' opposition to strategic bombing — is mainly quoted, most of Britain's church leaders supported the air offensive and the Archbishop of York, Dr Garbett, was reported as writing in the *York Diocesan Leaflet*: 'Often in life there is no clear choice between right and wrong; frequently the choice has to be made of the lesser of two evils, and it is a lesser evil to bomb a war-loving Germany than to sacrifice the lives of thousands of our own fellow-countrymen who long for peace and to delay delivering millions now held in slavery . . . However much we may deplore the sufferings of the civilian population and the destruction of their homes, and beautiful buildings, we must continue to use our superiority in the air as a means of ending the war as speedily as we can and then build up some strong central international order which will by force maintain peace until it is willingly accepted by all nations' — *The Times*, 25th June 1943. [6]

Judgements made by historians, commentators and the like, must surely be studied and conclusions sought within the time-frame in which the particular events were taking place and not based on current moral political correctness. Until the D-Day invasion in June 1944, Britain and her Allies had no means, apart from the strategic bomber, of taking the war to the Germans and to the Nazis in particular. No other means was available to bring home to the German nation the true horror of war: that horror which twice in the previous century they had inflicted on others as they laid waste to other countries. John Terraine quotes Dr Noble Frankland as saying to an audience at the Royal United Institute on the 13th December 1961, 'The great immorality open to us in 1940 and 1941 was to lose the war against Hitler's Germany. To have abandoned the only means of direct attack which we had at our disposal would have been a long step in that direction'.[7]

As pointed out earlier, Bomber Command was ill-prepared for the task that lay ahead when war broke out, largely due to the lack of foresight of all prewar political parties and the eagerness of all the organs of information to gull the general public into a state of inertia — exemplified by the *Express* newspaper banner headline on the very brink of the conflict: THERE AIN'T GONNA BE NO WAR.

Although Webster and Frankland did not say so, it appears that they also knew where the blame for Britain's ill-preparedness lay. 'The initial handicaps of Bomber Command as regards both its efficiency and its size were very severe and had prolonged effects. They were due to a combination of dilatoriness, financial stringency and the fact that air warfare was a new conception'.[8] Most of the available frontline aircraft were obsolescent, except for the Wellingtons, and the machines themselves were under-gunned; just ·303 machineguns against the Luftwaffe's aircraft cannons. They had a poor bombsight and worse, bombs, which more often than not did not explode. 'One fact less easy to explain or excuse was the performance of the bombs to be used by the Royal Air Force. This was inadequate in the First World War and at least as bad at the start of the next. The bomb, after all, is what bombing is all about. If the final link in the chain fails all others are meaningless'.[9]

A most sweeping statement, only partially true, as it could

131

be said that it applied only to the early years of the war, was published in the *Guinness Book of Military Blunders*, 'The low level of reliability of the bombs dropped by British aircraft during World War II meant that night after night over Germany half the crews of British bombers were risking their lives for nothing. They might as well have dropped baked bean cans. Official reports acknowledge that a third of all medium-capacity bombs broke up on impact or failed to detonate, while the picture was even worse in the case of high-capacity bombs or 'blockbusters'. If one adds the fact only one bomber in ten only got to within five miles of its target, that its bombs, when dropped, fell randomly over an area of 75 square miles, and then in 50 percent of cases failed to explode, one is obliged to call into question the competence of Bomber Command. It is a little known fact that during the bombing raids of 1940-1, more British fliers died than German civilians'. [10]

The criticism is frequently made that bombing did not prevent the increase of German war production. R J Overy in his book, *The Air War 1939-45*, says, 'But bombing was much more effective than the Allies believed. The important consequence of the bombing was not that it failed to stem the increase of arms production, but that it prevented the increase from being considerably greater than it was. Bombing placed a ceiling on German war production which was well below what Germany, with skilful and more urgent management of its resources, was capable of producing after 1943'.

Much is made about the RAF Bomber Command and the U.S. Eighth Air Force's manner of bombing. 'During the greater part of the war the one operated almost entirely at night and the other by day. This fact complicated the problem of concentration on one particular target system. It also complicates the problem of assessing the results produced by different methods of attack. But they were produced by a joint offensive and neither air force could have produced them by itself'. [11] The famous and often repeated remark is that the 'Norden' bombsight used by the Americans 'could put a bomb down a pickle barrel'. It sounds good but could only be achieved on a clear day, without flak or fighters to contend with.

'A bomb from 10,000 feet takes about 25 seconds to fall. In that time the aircraft has moved a mile or so, depending on the speed'. [12] The American bombers flew in a tight formation to ensure the maximum protection with the firepower of their ·5 guns. Whether the lead bomb-aimer could visually identify the target, or it could only be identified with radar, when he released his bombs the rest of the formation dropped theirs. Inevitably there would be one or two seconds delay between the formation bomb-aimers releasing their bombs after their bomb leader had dropped his, therefore an error of distance from the aiming point must occur. Thus the result of their bombing would be similar to that of Bomber Command, particularly when they were bombing by radar. The British aircraft bomb-aimers bombed targets individually.

It is not our intention in any way to denigrate the efforts nor the ability of the crews of the American Eighth USAAF. They pressed on with great determination and courage day after day against fighters and flak until they finally completed their tour of operations. Their British bomber colleagues certainly saluted their brothers in arms. But there is little doubt that there are many American historians and writers on this subject who are economical with the truth, when they compare British 'area' bombing and American 'precision' bombing. A Swiss military historian wrote, 'The American crews nevertheless exaggerated the degree of precision they could obtain with the Norden bombsight'. [13] Edward Jablenski, in his book *Flying Fortress* (page 112) wrote, 'While this method lacked precision it enabled the British to drop heavy bomb loads on the enemy. It was the

American belief that RAF's night area bombing was not economical nor as truly effective as the more precise daylight bombardment. The American strategies aimed at specific factories, marshalling yards and other targets which, if hit, would cripple the German economy. The British method of saturation bombing placed bombs in the general location of a military target area as well as the areas around it. The American method killed fewer civilians of course'.

'The US Army Air Forces stuck, in theory, to their 'precision' bombardments almost until the end of the European war. They wanted to become an independent service and therefore had to keep their 'sheet clean'. However, having suffered heavy losses over Germany in August and October 1943, they tried their first city attack, against Munster, in October. Their carpet bombing method (that is, the bomb release of entire combat boxes in synchronisation with leading plane) was never very accurate, and weather conditions as well as German defences accounted for further scattering of bombs over wide areas'. [14] Horst Boog also comments, 'As to bombing accuracy, Hays Parks has demonstrated in a recent study that Bomber Command had improved greatly and was often better than the US Army Air Forces' 'precision bombing', which was merely carpet bombing of selective targets'. [15]

British 'area' bombing was carried out with definite aiming points that were given at briefings prior to take off. Whereas the term 'carpet' bombing should strictly be applied to the USAAF and, with such deadly effect, to their Air Force when operating the B52 bombers in Vietnam. Thank goodness the technical advances since then have enabled the bomber forces to deliver explosives on selected targets using guidance systems that ensure a greater pinpoint accuracy.

'While Harris fought his great battles at night and made no attempt to conceal from the press or public the nature of area bombing, the USAAF in the winter of 1943/4 were forced to turn to area bombing. That winter, using H2X to bomb blind through cloud, the 8th Air Force achieved an average circular error of some 2 to 3 miles from the aiming point; this was comparable to the accuracy of the RAF at night. In the American Official History the historians say, "It seemed better to bomb low priority targets frequently, even with less than precision accuracy, than not to bomb at all". It would seem that the American historians have used less than precision accuracy themselves in attempting to conceal the American involvement in area bombing'! [16]

As is usual, some British historians and commentators have not been backward in denigrating what Bomber Command achieved. It is a favourite pastime in which the media are quick to join. The historian, A.J.P. Taylor wrote, '(by early 1945) . . . the strategic air offensive belatedly achieved decisive results. This was mainly the work of the Americans'. [17]

Notes, Chapter Eight

1. *Sunday Telegraph* – 29th April, 1984 Dudley Saward
2. *Tales from the Bombers,* Chaz Bowyer p240
3. *Before the Storm,* Robert Jackson p218
4. *The Spectator* – 4th February, 1985 Simon Jenkins
5. *Uncommon Valour,* A.G. Goulding p152
6. *Bombing Vindicated,* J.M. Spaight p118
7. *The Right of the Line,* John Terraine p683
8. *The Strategic Bomber Offensive Against Germany Vol 3,*
       Webster & Frankland p309

9. *The RAF and Two World Wars*, Sir Maurice Dean p306
10. *The Guinness Book of Military Blunders*, Geoffrey Regan p129
11. *Strategic Air Offensive Vol 1*, Webster & Frankland p31
12. *Bomber Pilot*, G/Capt L. Cheshire
13. *History of World War II*, Lt/Col Bauer p470
14. *Sir Arthur Harris Dispatch on War Operations*, Horst Boog xliii
15. *Sir Arthur Harris Dispatch on War Operations*, Horst Boog xlii
16. *Uncommon Valour*, A.G. Goulding p100
17. *English History 1914-1945*, A.J.P. Taylor p591

Chapter Nine

'It is not what we begin with, but what we end with'.

Unknown

SIR MICHAEL BEETHAM, GCB, CBE, DFC, AFC, DC, wrote the following in his Introduction to *The Bomber Battle of Berlin* by A/Cdr John Searby DSO, DFC, MRAF: 'The bombing offensive against Germany in the Second World War was unique in that for the first time such a method of waging war, independent of action on land and sea had been attempted. Much controversy has surrounded the Bomber Offensive both over the targets selected for attack and whether on its own, given more resources, it could have forced the surrender of Germany. What is much more evident is that without the Offensive and its contribution to achieving air superiority, Operation Overlord would not have been mounted at all'.

So to use the modern parlance, what was the bottom line?

The Butcher's Bill (as the Navy used to term those who were killed after a naval engagement in the nineteenth century) was heavy; but then so was the Battle of the Somme in the Great War. Aircrew were all volunteers and, it was said, were the flower of British youth. Despite the losses, volunteers still came forward from the beginning of the war to its end and there can be little doubt the country lost, in their self-sacrifice, a generation of fine prospective leaders.

This was after all, the first time that strategic bombers as a fighting force had operated. So what criteria could be used to judge whether the Bomber Offensive was successful? There has been much negative reporting, often coloured by the individual's own preconceived ideas. John Keegan, the *Daily Telegraph* Military Editor, has written (*History of Warfare*), 'Strategic bombing had not defeated Germany. The manned bomber was a fragile weapon of offensive. There is no acceptance that it had made a major contribution on land or sea as well as in the air'. This is the judgement of a man with close connections with the Army.

Professor Patrick Blackett, educated at Osborne and Dartmouth, served in the Navy during the First World war, was later director of Operations and Research at the Admiralty and has been described by Sir Maurice Dean as 'an outstanding man of science well versed in military and especially in naval matters'. In an article for the *Scientific American* in April 1961 the Professor wrote: 'No part of the war effort has been so well documented as the (bombing) campaign, which had as its official objective "the destruction and dislocation of the German military, industrial and economic system and the undermining of the morale of the German people to the point where their capacity for armed resistance is fatally weakened" . . . Without any doubt the area bombing offensive was an expensive failure'. [1]

The question of area bombing has always been used as a means of attacking Harris's judgement. It has already been illustrated that there was little difference between the American and British bombing techniques. 'The American Official History has been largely responsible for post-war generations believing it was Harris of Bomber Command who was solely responsible for the area bombing of German cities. The truth is the American commanders matched Harris ruin for ruin over Germany.

Spaatz was perfectly willing to commit his bomber force to bombing cities, but always ensured some window dressing was provided such as 'blind bombing of transportation centres'. . . General Eaker in a letter to Spaatz dated 1st January 1945 and quoted by the American Historians said

"We should never allow the history of this war to convict us of throwing the strategic bomber at the man in the street.'" [2]

It is obvious the Americans are a lot better at being economical with the interpretation of facts than their British cousins. Bomber Command was forced into area bombing because of the demonstrable limitations of early navigational aids and bomb-aiming equipment. The precision bombing techniques pioneered by the Pathfinder Force were developed with such outstanding success much later in the war, just prior to the D-Day invasion and, subsequently, when assisting the Armies.

BOMBER COMMAND'S SEA OPERATIONS

MINING

Harris had studied the question of laying sea mines from the air when he was Deputy Director (Plans) before the war. After the outbreak of war as the AOC 5 Group, which operated the Hampden bomber, he had put his theories into practice, and mining became a major campaign when he took over Bomber Command in 1942.

'The air mining campaign sank 717 merchant vessels and damaged another 665 . . . In addition, mines laid by Bomber Command — which totalled over 47,000 during the war — had important strategic effects at critical times. They delayed the emergence of U-boats from their Biscay bases during the TORCH and OVERLORD operations; and in 1944 they drove the new large U-boats from their Bay of Danzig training waters, and so helped to ruin Admiral Dönitz's chances of operating them in significant numbers before the end of the war . . .

'Though the attacks on the Biscay bases in 1942 achieved little, the later bombing of Hamburg, Bremen, Kiel, Emden and other German ports, as well as the Dortmund-Ems Canal, achieved a great deal. In this the USAAF was fully associated, as it also was in attacks on inland towns manufacturing U-boat components. According to the British Bombing Survey, Bomber Command and the USAAF between them destroyed 111 U-boats in production and sank 54 which had been delivered to the German Navy'. [3]

BOMBING

'U-boats sunk at sea 1, sunk by bombing in port 21, sunk by air laid mines 17'. [4]

'New larger U-boats were to be built at inland factories where, in addition, engines and electrical equipment were also to be installed. They were then to be transported in sections to the coast to be assembled there and to complete their equipment in the shipyards . . . Forty-four of these U-boats were, in fact, destroyed in the shipyards between January and March 1945 . . .

The British Bombing Survey Unit in its report on 'The Effects of Strategic Bombing on the Production of German U-Boats' states that from May 1943 until the end of March 1945 the losses of U-Boats caused by the bombing of Germany were:-

Production losses: 111
Sinkings: 42
Total: 153

These figures include the forty-four destroyed between January and March 1945, mentioned above. They also include the 21 U-boats destroyed by Bomber Command referred to . . . The total losses of 153 U-boats . . . cannot, of course, all be credited to Bomber Command. A substantial percentage must certainly be ascribed to the US Eighth Bomber Command. Nevertheless Bomber Command was unquestionably responsible for 50 per cent at the very least; and it is probable that the percentage is a great deal higher than this'. [5]

'The bombing of enemy Capital ships had the following results: -

Tirpitz, Scheer, Lützow	Sunk.
Schlesian	Mined and beached.
Gneisenau	Held up in Brest by bombing from March 1941, to February 1942; mined; bombed, partially gutted; finally dismantled.
Köln	Damaged by bombs in Oslo Fjord; sunk by US Eighth Air Force in Wilhelmshaven where she had been forced to return for repairs.
Hipper	Severely damaged by bombs in dry dock at Kiel; rendered out of action for rest of war.
Sharnhorst	Held up in Brest by bombing from March 1941 to February 1942; mined and severely damaged on return to Kiel; finally sunk by Navy.
Prinz Eugen	Damaged by bombs and kept out of action for a year.
Emden	Damaged by bombs at Kiel, beached and burnt out.

Quite apart from these successes, the *Prinz Eugen* and the *Nürnberg* would have undoubtedly been sunk at Copenhagen during the last week of the war but for the fact that the attacking No 5 Group aircraft were recalled on representations made by the Admiralty. No explanation was given. Copenhagen suffered bombardment by these ships the very next day.' [6]

'A few days after D-Day there was an urgent call to destroy the enemy's large fleet of E boats and other light naval craft in the Channel which the Navy thought an extremely serious threat to the invading army's sea communications'. [7] Harris arranged attacks on Le Havre and Boulogne on June 14-15th. He wrote, 'There could be no more convincing demonstration of air power than these two operations . . . At Le Havre very nearly every ship in dock, more than 60 all told were sunk or damaged, and at Boulogne 28 vessels were sunk and many others damaged. In all, some 130 naval and auxiliary craft were put out of action, virtually the whole of the enemy's light naval forces in the Channel area'. [8]

'Taking account of Bomber Command successes in the 'Battle of the Ships', it is surprising that the Admiralty virtually ignored Harris's efforts and showed little, if indeed any, appreciation'. [9] It is also forgotten that in the Battle of Britain, 'Bomber Command's attacks in September 1940 on the French and Belgian Channel ports and the barges mustered there compelled the Germans to disperse their craft'. [10]

CO-OPERATION WITH THE ALLIED ARMIES

Prior to D-Day, a Transportation Plan was drawn up. It was a comprehensive strategy for the destruction of every key rail link in Northern France, 'On the night of the actual invasion the Command was out in great strength attacking gun emplacements, radar installations, etc'. [11] Other squadrons were used to drop WINDOW to confuse enemy radar in the Pas de Calais area and also off the coast of Boulogne. These spoof raids gave an illusion of massed shipping approaching other coasts on the enemy radar screens that certainly assisted the actial seaborne invasion of Normandy. In July, Harris wrote to the Chief of Air Staff complaining that his crews were not receiving sufficient recognition for their achievements; 'It was not known to the British people that, in making their tremendous effort in support of the Allied Armies, Bomber Command's casualties in the first weeks after D Day were higher than those of the British Second Army in Normandy'. [12]

Harris wrote that, 'tactical bombing of the German lines of communication was very far from our sole commitment. Within a few days of the landing in Normandy we were called upon to take part in a long campaign against German synthetic oil plants in Germany and, as soon as the first flying bombs were launched, to give very high priority to the new flying bomb launching sites and supply depots in the Pas de Calais'. [13]

The Command was frequently called on to assist the Army. At Caen the British and Canadian Armies could make little headway, and the strategic bombers were called upon. However there were some who complained that the resulting bomb craters and collapsed buildings stopped the armour from getting through. Harris commented, 'when our armour did go forward 24 hours later, the first objectives were taken with scarcely a struggle, the enemy in the front line being still in complete confusion. But after the initial success, the armour did not push on'. [14]

Montgomery, who was not a man to hand out praise very often, wrote to Harris after the air attacks on enemy concentrations around Caen: 'Again the Allied Armies in France would like to thank you personally and Bomber

143

Command for your magnificent co-operation last night. We know well that your main work was further afield and we applaud your continuous and sustained bombing of German war industries and the effect this has on the German war effort. But we also know well that you are always ready to bring your mighty effort closer in when such action is really needed and to co-operate in our tactical battle'. [15]

Further assistance was required from time to time. The action at the Falaise Gap being one such occasion.

In June, Bomber Command was asked to bomb synthetic oil plants in conjunction with the Americans. Harris had of course, already been bombing some of those plants which were situated in the Ruhr. It is well documented that Harris did not like what he called 'panacea targets', in which he included oil. Despite his arguments, 'He was overruled, but even after Bomber Command had, by the end of September, dropped 16,176 tons on oil targets, he still remained of that view'. [16]

Nevertheless as Bomber Command continued to bomb oil targets, 'if Speer is to be believed, the attacks made on these plants by night by Bomber Command were more effective than any made by day either by that Command or by the Americans, the reason — according to him — being that (by the British) much heavier bombs were used. Another reason was the greater accuracy achieved at night.

'This may sound paradoxical; it is not. In daylight it was rare for more than the first formation of the assaulting force to see the target, which immediately became obscured by the dust and smoke caused by the bombs being dropped. Thus it was very difficult, if not impossible, for the formations following behind to attack with accuracy . . .

'By February, 1945, Bomber Command had reached the huge figure of 62,339 tons of bombs cast down on oil targets. In March and April it added a further 24,289 tons. Yet, if Speer is to be believed, the vital damage to the synthetic oil plants had been caused much earlier by the 9,941 tons dropped upon them in the first half of 1944. Slightly more than half of these had fallen from aircraft of the United States Eighth Air Force operating in daylight'. [17]

'Between D Day and the end of war in Europe Bomber Command efforts were divided roughly as follows:-

Area bombing	32%
Military Targets	28%
Oil	17%
Transportation	15%
Navel Targets	3%
Airfields and Aircraft Industry	2%
Other	3%

The figure for military targets covers military installations as well as direct support to the land forces'. [18]

Norman Longmate in his assessment states, 'At the end of the war in Europe the strength of Bomber Command stood at ninety-five squadrons compared with the thirty-three much weaker ones with which it had started the war. The average number of aircraft available on any day had risen from 280 in September 1939 to 1609 in April 1945. 1,440 of these were four-engined bombers and the rest Mosquitoes, and they could carry 9000 tons of bombs to Berlin compared to a mere 456 tons back in September 1939'. [19]

Hilary St G. Saunders concludes, 'The fact that had Germany not been devastated with fire and high explosive and had not her industries in the process melted away, she must have won the war. For she would inevitably have been able to build a bomber fleet and to have wrought far greater destruction than she in fact achieved . . . That she would have done so without scruple or pity can reasonably be inferred from the action taken by the Luftwaffe in the days of strength against Warsaw, Rotterdam and Belgrade, and, for that matter, London'. [20] In the graph opposite he illustrates how Bomber Command, joining subsequently with the 8th US Air Force, had the tonnage of bombs rising steadily, peaking in 1944 and thus hastening the demise of the Nazi regime. To arrive at definitive figures of bombs dropped by Bomber Command and the 8th U.S.A.A.F. is not easy, Webster and Frankland admit in Vol 4 of *The Strategic Bombing Offensive Against Germany 1939 - 1945* (published 1963) they studied several sources before making their final assessment. Adding the monthly figures quoted on pages 455/457, the sum total of these annual figures show — 955,044 tons were dropped by Bomber Command and 623,438 by the 8th U.S.A.A.F. This final figure of 955,044 for Bomber Command tallies with the statistics quoted in Table 1 (page 44) of *Sir Arthur T. Harris, Dispatch on War Operations 1942-1945*. Who knows what might have happened if such tonnages could have been dropped when war broke out.

'In the last year of the war Bomber Command played a major part in the almost complete destruction of whole vital parts of German oil production, in the virtual dislocation of her communication system and in the elimination of other important activities. Moreover, the continuing area offensive, apart from assuming almost unmanageable proportions in many towns, contributed important by-products to the achievement of the main plans for oil and transport. These direct results had a decisive effect upon the outcome of the war and there were also continuing and accelerating indirect results which were scarcely less important. Moreover, this was achieved in spite of massive diversions of force to the direct support of the armies and of the navies'. [21]

The German Reich Minister of Armaments and War Production, Albert Speer who was interrogated after the war, subsequently wrote two books. He made many observations

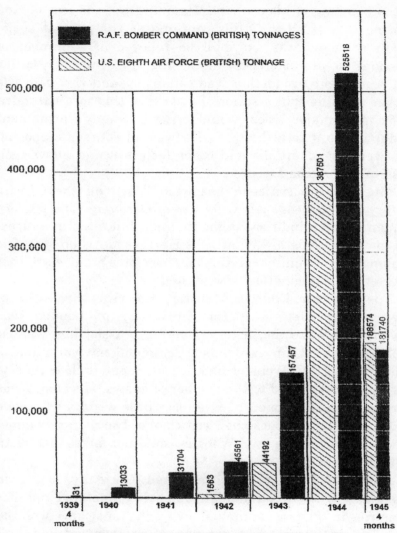

**ANNUAL TONNAGES OF BOMBS DROPPED BY THE R.A.F.
BOMBER COMMAND AND THE U.S. EIGHTH AIR FORCE, 1939-1945**

147

on the bombing of his country, 'Hamburg put the fear of God into me . . . If all air raids continue at the present scale, within three months we shall be relieved of a number of questions we are at present discussing . . . I informed Hitler that armament production was collapsing and threw in the further warning that a series of attacks of this sort, extended to six more major cities, would bring Germany's armament production to a total halt'. [22] He was, of course, supposing that weather conditions and other factors would allow such massive raids to be executed.

'Much of the criticism has been based on the Official History *The Strategic Air Offensive of Germany*. The History frequently in an indirect, veiled manner, but often in a direct and more immediate way, attacks Harris's views on strategic bombing, his handling of the bomber force, and says that much of the bomber effort was wasted . . .

'The late Sir Charles Webster, Emeritus Professor of International History at the University of London was appointed to write the history. Chosen to assist him was Dr Noble Frankland, an ex-Bomber Command navigator and a holder of the DFC. Webster had already made it clear that he was violently opposed to the bomber offensive. His choice was therefore a curious one . . . Even so, those writers who have used the History to back their criticism of Harris rarely quote some passages which even Webster could not fail to include in his balance sheet:

(Such as) "The fact is that had Germany not been devastated with fire and high explosive, and had not her industries in the process melted away, she must have won the war . . . In turning the weapon of air war against her, therefore, the pilots and crews of Bomber Command were as much the saviours of their country as the pilots of Fighter Command in the Battle of Britain".

'The History also concludes that: "Both cumulatively in largely indirect ways and eventually in a more immediate and direct manner, strategic bombing and, also in other roles strategic bombers, made a contribution to victory which was decisive'". [23]

Three basic questions require an answer:-

1 Did the Royal Air Force as a separate fighting force fulfil the expectations of its founder in 1917?

An unbiased conclusion must surely be in the affirmative, even if it did take time to receive the necessary navigation and bombing aids; and to learn the techniques, which would eventually ensure the success of the strategic bombers in waging war.

2 Did the operational division of the three major commands, namely Fighter, Bomber and Coastal make a significant contribution overall; at the same time giving the necessary assistance to the other two services?

Undoubtedly. Fighter Command in the Battle of Britain; Coastal Command in the war at sea by co-operating with the Navy and successfully finding and sinking many U-boats; the strategic Bomber Force by taking the war to the enemy's homeland and slowing their productive capacity and, when the time finally arrived, giving the fullest possible support to the land and sea forces both during and after the landings in Normandy.

3 Did Bomber Command justify the expenditure of the 7 per cent it is said it was allocated, and used, from the war economy?

It has already been mentioned that the original lack of funding during the inter-war years held back research and the build-up of squadron strength. But of even greater significance, 'the instability of air doctrine lay in the fact that air forces were compelled to make guesses about how aircraft

149

would be used once war had actually broken out. There was little experience to draw on about the kind of air war most powers expected to fight, so that much air doctrine was an act of faith that the guesses of one particular air force were the right ones'. [24]

When war finally broke out, Bomber Command had to learn the hard way, but, it did learn the essential lessons, and with the co-operation of the scientific establishment by the end of 1943, the bombers were able to find, mark and bomb successfully, in spite of most weather conditions. They successfully met the requirements of the Navy and in so doing sank many enemy vessels; they fought as a tactical force to further the objectives of the land forces.

Finally "Bomber" Harris, the Commander-in-Chief, fought his corner, perhaps with exaggeration at times — but with humour — to bring about an early end to the fighting and loss of Allied lives.

Although Churchill had always encouraged the bombing programme on numerous occasions, he started to distance himself after the Dresden raid. In his victory speech he made just a brief reference to Bomber Command saying he wished to express a deep sense of gratitude for what Bomber Command had achieved under his (Harris's) direction. This for public consumption. However Charles Messenger quotes a private letter from Churchill to Harris, dated 15th May 1945, in which he lists Bomber Commands achievements and concludes, 'I believe that the massive achievements of Bomber Command will long be remembered as an example of duty nobly done'. [25]

Even so Harris was denied the publication of his Final Order of the Day when peace was declared. It was published in the Pathfinder Magazine, *The Marker*, Winter 1990, see appendix C.

Harris fought hard for the members of his Command to be

given a campaign medal, not just for his aircrews, but for the devotion and the sacrifice of the ground staff to be recognised — nearly nine thousand died. The men and women on the ground worked in all weathers, on airfields blasted by freezing winds. In the bitter wartime winters, often in drenching rain or thick fog; the engine fitters some 20 feet up on scaffolding, armourers, electricians, wireless and radar mechanics all labouring round the clock to keep the bombers airworthy. Recognition was of course denied them, which made Harris very angry, and as a final snub, both he and the Pathfinder Chief, Don Bennett were left out of the Victory Honours. Such is political cowardice.

In the *Daily Telegraph*, 15th May 1988 — a précis of the Last Volume of the Official Life of Churchill, by Martin Gilbert, Part 1, was published. Towards the end of the article part of a letter from Churchill to Attlee, written January 6th 1946, included this sentence, 'When we consider the immense part played by the bombing offensive in shortening the war and thus bringing it to an end before the enemy long range weapons developed their full potency, nobody can deny its cardinal importance'.

Harris never seemed troubled by what was written or said about him, seldom replying to the criticism in public or correspondence; but he was fiercely defensive of his 'old lags' of Bomber Command when the occasion arose.

The role, contribution and success of Bomber Command to the overall war effort has been expressed throughout this book, but here are some other people's conclusions:

'The part played by Bomber Command in the winning of the war did justify the 7 per cent of the national war effort it absorbed and much of the credit of this must go to Harris himself, especially, in his dogged upholding of that principle of war, maintenance of the aim, and his ability to inspire those under him to carry it out'. [26]

'If the air marshals had pitched their demands for

resources, their own hopes and their subsequent claims more modestly, history might have judged them more kindly. As it was, the cost of the bomber offensive in life, treasure and moral superiority over the enemy tragically outstripped the results it achieved'. [27]

In the chapter entitled, *The Achievements and the Post War Critics*, James Hampton (who was the sole survivor of three brothers who served in Bomber Command), sums it up perfectly, with a straightforward assessment of the many critics who have expressed their views since the war. For example, 'The strategic bomber offensive against the German economy was essentially a war of attrition. Therefore, and in the nature of things, there were no spectacular victories with the equivalents of army commanders offering to surrender. This is a great pity if only because of the large number of people who are unable to recognise a victory unless it is accompanied by white flags. Generals with bowed heads and long lines of prisoners trudging into incarceration'. [28] He concludes the chapter, 'It therefore seems likely that the verdict of history will be that there was no alternative strategy; also, that the bomber offensive had as decisive an effect on the outcome of the war as was within the power of Britain to achieve, no matter how else the resources in manpower and equipment devoted to it might have been used'. [29] That seems to be a fair summing up.

Richard Overy, who writes an acid criticism of Bomber Command and its early failures, says in his concluding remarks in the chapter *Bombers and Bombing*, 'for all the arguments over the morality or operational effectiveness of the bombing campaigns, the air offensive was one of the decisive elements in Allied victory'. [30]

'If historians have dealt with Harris and Bomber Command rather unfairly and harshly, they cannot deny that those raids brought home to Germany, as nothing else could have done, the real meaning of the war they started'. [31]

'The bearing of those who saw active service with Bomber Command was that of the whole Royal Air Force . . . whether in battle against the Luftwaffe, in attacking targets in Occupied Europe or the German Reich, or quartering the skies above a convoy driving along the perilous paths of the ocean, they deployed a mastery which was the admiration of the world and saved the course of freedom'. [32]

'The airmen, who since the war, have pointed out to the historians that they thought the bomber offensive was being sold short in the history books were more or less told they were overstating their cases. However, I have noticed as time goes on there appears to be a wind of change in the historians' attitude and much more credit is now being given to the achievements of the bomber offensive'. [33]

There can be no doubt that the Royal Air Force has earned its right to be an independent force to defend Britain and her interests when under attack, and to co-operate with the other two services as and when required. 'I am utterly convinced that the outstanding and vital lesson of this last war is that air power is the dominant factor in this modern world and that, though the methods of exercising it will change it will remain the dominant factor as long as air power determines the fate of nations . . . and that sea power properly exercised can still be one of the keys to our country and not merely a commitment'. [34]

As this is being written, two newspapers have published articles. In *The Observer,* 15th February 1998, a headline read 'History damned "Bomber" Harris on the word of his arch-enemy', with a sub-heading, 'On the basis of a single jaundiced report — by his rival Solly Zuckerman . . . Sir Arthur Harris has been reviled for 50 years'. The piece, written by Pete Beaumont and Dennis Staunton, discussed the publication of the British Bombing Survey Unit and a commentary by Sebastian Cox. I quote 'Cox believes his work will overturn decades of presumptions by historians that

Harris's attachment to area bombing of German cities was doubly immoral in that it had no effect on the Nazi war effort. He argues that the portrayal of area bombing as a failure in the British Bombing Survey Unit was far from dispassionate. Written by "Solly" (later Lord) Zuckerman, one of Harris's greatest opponents on area bombing, the report was, according to Cox, fundamentally inaccurate and clouded by Zuckerman's own obsessions. For years Zuckerman's report has been regarded as proof of the callous pointlessness of the strategy. But Zuckerman . . . was far from neutral . . . and every bit as egotistical as Harris . . . The gist of the argument says Cox, "is that Zuckerman's claims over the effect of area bombing on the German economy was very much underestimated. The bombing had a considerable effect on the German war effort". Cox does not believe Zuckerman was deliberately trying to blacken Harris's name; he thinks Zuckerman was simply unable to accept that he might be wrong.'

The *Daily Telegraph* on 16th February 1998, had a column by Will Bennett entitled, "Bomber" Harris's name 'was blighted by rival'. It states that, 'Sebastian Cox, an official at the Air Historical Branch at the Ministry of Defence and a leading expert on the RAF's bombing offensive during the Second World War has written a commentary in the British Bombing Survey Unit report which had not been published but made available to historians, and was now to be published for the general public . . . 'Mr Cox revealing that it was written by Zuckerman, although it was never attributed to him.' It concludes, 'other recently discovered evidence has also helped to rehabilitate Harris — German reports show that production of tanks, aircraft and trucks had dropped drastically because of the bombing campaign and one third of output was devoted to anti-aircraft guns to counter the raids'.

So it has taken all this time for the truth to out.

The late C-in-C Bomber Command, Sir Arthur Travers Harris GCB, OBE, AFC, should take his place among the great commanders of the British forces; for his blunt, unwavering determination against criticism and his outstanding leadership, so inspiring to the people in his Command.

It is a typically British trait to denigrate people in the public eye whenever possible and to belittle their achievements. Certainly many of our journalists, columnists and writers do not always thoroughly research their subject and sometimes allow their conclusions to be coloured by their particular prejudices.

It is for you, the reader, to make your own judgement.

Notes, Chapter Nine

1. *RAF and Two World Wars,* Sir Maurice Dean p292
2. *Uncommon Valour,* A.G. Goulding p152
3. *Hardest Victory,* Denis Richards p298/9
4. *Bomber Harris,* Dudley Saward p315
5. *Bomber Harris,* Dudley Saward p317/318
6. *Bomber Harris,* Dudley Saward p316/317
7. *Bomber Offensive,* Sir Arthur Harris p209
8. *Bomber Offensive,* Sir Arthur Harris p210
9. *Bomber Harris,* Dudley Saward p318
10. *Hardest Victory,* Denis Richards p298
11. *Uncommon Valour,* A.G. Goulding p138
12. *Uncommon Valour,* A.G. Goulding p140
13. *Bomber Offensive,* Sir Arthur Harris p209

14. *Bomber Offensive,* Sir Arthur Harris p211

15. *Bomber Offensive,* Sir Arthur Harris p213

16. *The RAF 1939-1945 Book 3,* Hilary St G. Saunders p260

17. *The RAF 1939-1945 Book 3,* Hilary St G. Saunders p268

18. *RAF and Two World Wars,* Sir Maurice Dean p285

19. *The Bombers,* Norman Longmate p348

20. *The RAF 1939-1945 Book 3,* Hilary St G. Saunders p388/389

21. *The Strategic Air Offensive Against Germay Vol 3,*
       Webster & Frankland p288/289

22. *Inside the Third Reich,* Albert Speer p284

23. *Uncommon Valour,* A.G. Goulding p156-158

24. *The Air War.* R.J. Overy p17

25. *Bomber Harris,* Charles Messenger p197

26. *Bomber Harris,* Charles Messenger p214

27. *Bomber Command,* Max Hastings p424

28. *Selected for Aircrew,* James Hampton p318/319

29. *Selected for Aircrew,* James Hampton p341

30. *Why the Allies Won the War,* Richard Overy p133

31. *Flypast June 84. Tribute to Sir Arthur Harris,* Francois Prins

32. *The RAF 1939-1945 Book 3,* Hilary St G. Saunders p393

33. *Through The Bomb Sight,* Andrew Maitland p182/183

34. *Air Power in War,* Lord Tedder p123

Chapter Ten

'What a society gets in its armed services is exactly what is asked for no more no less. What it asks for tends to be a reflection of what it is. When a country looks at its fighting forces it is looking in a mirror; the mirror is a true one and the faces it sees its own'.

General Sir John Hackett

THIS BOOK HAS NOT SET OUT TO BE A POLITICAL tract, but to record the views and written opinions of others, especially those who served in the RAF, and in Bomber Command in particular, in the Second World War. It has seemed to me to be only fair to give those who served not only their country but Western civilisation itself an opportunity to answer some of the critics who have frequently denigrated that service by ill-informed judgements based on poor research or pre-conceived ideas, liberally coloured by hindsight and the vacuities of political correctness.

Now, armed with lessons learned from the past, it is time to look to the future.

The world today is a much more dangerous place than it was before the Second World War. Then there were three or four malign despots. Now there are many more. Totalitarian states have risen and fallen in the last fifty years, but many endure — often controlled by bigoted fanatics prepared to do anything to maintain their hold on the levers of power.

Just consider the betrayal of human rights in many African countries whose economies were in good heart when they obtained independence and which have been reduced to mass starvation and penury either by self-styled 'Generals' or

157

'Colonels' hungry for rapine and riches as they waged endless civil wars or else by cynical 'Presidents' with secret fat offshore bank accounts.

Consider also what has happened in Asia, Korea, Vietnam and in Pol Pot's 'killing fields' of Cambodia. Consider what *is* happening in the Middle East now.

Over the years the United Nations has tried — with varying degrees of success — to defuse tense international situations and avoid conflict; but as Field Marshal Jan Smuts once said, 'Peace unbacked by power, remains a dream'. It can therefore, only be left to the democratic countries of the world to band together, each nation's duty to be militarily strong, acting together to foil the machinations of those, who can and do bring chaos, misery and death to many of their wretched countrymen.

The nations of the world still fall far short of the ideals set out in the Atlantic Charter and the Charter of Human Rights, agreed in the Second World War, probably the two most important international documents drawn up this century. Constant vigilance and pressure from the international community is necessary if ever those ideals are to be fulfilled.

The first duty of any government, regardless of its political persuasion, is to ensure the safety and security of its citizens, which is necessarily linked to a high degree of preparedness of its Armed Forces and the supremacy of their equipment. Good Social Services or the best National Health Service in the world, will not ensure any nation's independence of action, or defence of its people if threatened. The study of history gives sufficient evidence that our own so-called Continental partners are not the most reliable when under pressure, and have usually put their own interests first. It was General de Gaulle who said, 'The British are European, but not Continental'. Over the centuries, this country has fought for certain democratic principles and offered refuge to the genuine refugees fleeing from oppression, usually from

European countries. Now it must define where its moral obligations lie and where its wealth is best spent.

Marshal of the Royal Air Force, Lord Tedder declared 'It would be a singularly futile business for us, having been brought uncomfortably near bankruptcy by two world wars on the blank cheque basis, to complete the journey to the bankruptcy court by uncritical defence expenditure in peace'. [1]

Britain has been likened to a giant aircraft carrier, anchored off the continental landmass, and when the phrase 'balance forces', repeatedly made by the so-called experts is used, it is really a misleading expression. In any case, experience teaches one to be wary of 'experts', invariably they exist on both sides of a debate; common sense is the quality most required.

It would seem that this country does not require large continental style land forces. Indeed prior to the Napoleonic wars, the Navy used to transport the Army to where its presence was judged to be most needed, although, no doubt, greater success could have been achieved on occasions if the Generals and the Admirals had not been so jealous of their respective positions.

The 20th century has seen the greatest advance in scientific discovery, research and technology of any previous age. So rapid have been the advances, that almost every aspect of life has been affected. Unfortunately, whilst in many cases the developments have enhanced the quality of life, so also have they resulted in bringing great suffering and hardship to many people. No doubt there will be even greater discoveries in this present century. Mankind's inbuilt inquisitiveness and almost overwhelming desire to act as God is never stilled. The study of history shows that the human race is so acquisitive, aggressive and greedy that an excuse can always be found to start a conflict. The past century was no exception and with the help of science, two world wars have taken the lives of millions of people around the globe as well as brought immense suffering and deprivation to countless survivors.

In considering the future of our country it is essential that we avoid the divisions that bedevilled relations between the Military and Naval establishments and the Royal Air Force between the wars. Regretfully even now there still seems to be indications of inter-service rivalry and wrangling from time to time. Whilst recognising that the Armed Forces were ill prepared for battle prior to World War II, due as much to such inter-service argument as to financial stringency, there is now ample evidence to establish that the ability to apply air power in all its phases, for both defence and offence, is vital if air supremacy is to be obtained at the outset. Already it is possible to see similarities between the betrayals of the 1930's defence reviews, and the envisaged cutbacks currently hidden beneath the gobbledegook of fast talking government ministers and their spin doctors. Many lessons, so harshly learnt, seem to have been forgotten. The need to have an available weapon of air power and the ability to wield it has been demonstrated to be vital not only in the last war, but also in the conflicts since.

As an island, the first requirement for us must be a strong Air Force, able to defend our shores, to give aid and cover to the other Services as required, yet to still have the ability to take the attack to any future enemy's homeland. Lord Trenchard wrote, 'Air power can dispense with the intermediate step, can pass over . . . enemies armies and air defences and attack directly the centres of productivity, transportation and communications from which the enemy war effort is maintained'. With today's advances in guidance systems this is a proven statement.

In any future conflict our country will not have the dubious luxury of two or three years in which to equip the Air Force with the right type of aircraft and the latest weaponry to enable it to carry out its appointed task.

As for the other services, Lord Tedder wrote in the *Sunday Express*, October 1948, 'Sea power remained, as it still remains, vital to our very existence, but the forces required to express sea power have changed in character'. It follows, therefore, that a strong Navy must also be preserved, with two or possibly three aircraft carriers and with an adequate screen of ships and supply vessels to protect them.

Turning to the Army, it should be streamlined and given the most up-to-date equipment as it becomes available, thus ensuring its mobility and its ability to attack. Constant research should be carried out; as, for example, to discover whether helicopter gunships would have a greater punch in attack than tanks. Here is a case for 'balancing forces'.

To be sure that there is a 'force in training'. Able to rapidly expand and strengthen front line troops, as and when required, the Territorial Army should be kept at maximum strength. Equally, every effort including funding, should be made to encourage interest and recruitment to the Cadet Corps of the three Services, for these young people are the seed corn of the future. Moreover it will give them comradeship and a taste of discipline, coupled with self-discipline and self-reliance. These qualities will be essential to the men and women in the Armed Forces in the world of the twenty first century.

So it will cost money! Your money, provided by the taxpayer, not as is so often stated when spending is mentioned by ministers and commentators that 'Government money will be used'. Government has no money. Every penny it spends is yours.

Why should it be that when our country goes to war our Armed Forces, only then, almost invariably discover shortages and inadequacies in their equipment, often resulting in unnecessary casualties because of bad decisions made by 'shiny trousered, chairborne wonders'. It is time that the hoary old saying, 'we always lose every battle but the last', was put to rest. Our Armed Forces should be maintained at peak readiness for action, and with the best available equipment, at all times. The cost might be high, but in these perilous times it would be a reasonable and necessary expense, in sharp contrast to other more politically correct ways governments have of lavishly spending our money.

Geoffrey Regan, in the Introduction to *The Guinness Book of Military Blunders* writes, 'Villains there have been and butchers too. But often these men have been shielded from the horrors of front-line fighting by distance or telephone lines or concrete bunkers. Sometimes the blunderers have been planners, who have sent men into battle ill-equipped, badly clothed or unfed. They have sent them to fight in deserts, in mountains made impassable by snow, in swamps, or in disease-ridden jungles. They have asked men, and their generals, to do things that were impossible, and when the casualty lists have been collected they have blamed the commanders and frontline soldiers for failings that were rightly theirs.

'And seated in leather chairs, behind oak desks and in panelled offices, sit the politicians, the deputies of the people, in whose name the slaughter is committed. Only visiting quiet areas of the front, distanced from the consequences of their policies by the filtering presence of staff officers and commanders desperate to impress, it is easy for the politician to forget that he deals in death just as surely as the man who gives the order to attack. His mistakes are every bit as costly as the general's and his motives frequently far more cynical. If the military Saul has slain his thousands, the political David has certainly slain his ten thousands, and frequently with far less cause'. [2]

If Britain wishes to retain any influence in world affairs and to hold its rightful place in the Security Council of the United Nations, it is essential that Britain leads from strength and example, and not rhetoric.

Only you, the reader can make the final judgement and act accordingly.

To repeat the words of Field Marshal Jan Smuts, **'Peace unbacked by power remains a dream'.**

Notes, Chapter Ten

1. *Air Power in War,* Lord Tedder p27
2. *Guiness Book of Military Blunders,* Geoffrey Regan, Introduction

Epilogue

6 September 1998, *The Independent on Sunday*, publishing an article by Michael Ignatieff on The UN's Genocide Convention passed fifty years ago, including these words, 'Dresden's people were citizens of a state waging exterminatory war; the bombing was an act of war. Once the conflict ended, the bombing ceased. It was as just a war as ever was fought, but its justice does not justify war crimes. And a war crime Dresden certainly was: indiscriminate slaughter of a civilian population for no military or tactical objective, or none that can be subsequently defended. That no one was punished is an inequity of victor's justice. But injustice is not undone by misdescribing the crime.'

The comments on Dresden do not agree with information that has become available under the thirty-year rule. Dresden was not only a major communication centre on the Eastern front, but also a vital railhead for German troops arriving on the Russian front. It should be remembered it had many large important armament factories, despite the Nazi claims to the contrary that they were only producing tooth paste and baby powder. The tragedy was conditions turned out to be tactically ideal, unlike the majority of bombing operations that were hindered by weather or lack of equipment. Although it resulted in many thousands of civilian lives to be lost it seemed to prove the air lobby's claim that air power could and would, in the long run, save allied lives in any future conflicts.

In recent years it has been common practice to grub around destroying reputations and/or altering events in history, to allow dramatic licence when presenting a block busting film or play, so that the unwary tend to accept the offerings as a 'true record', or when challenged the authors hide behind the phrase, 'The need to know.'

Present and future generations are in danger of having quite a false picture of the past presented, especially when the phrase, 'We *should apologise*' for this or that event which has taken place over the centuries. History is there to be learnt and to be learned from. It is a subject that has a very low priority in the school curriculum, particularly British history. We should stand up and be proud of our, the British, contribution for democracy and the example we set in leading the fight for freedom in World Wars.

Even to the present day, and as you read this book, commentators will continue to use Dresden to slate Bomber Command instead of looking at the wider picture . . .

Bomber Command

**125,000 aircrew flew
of whom**

**55,500 were killed
and
9,838 became Prisoners-of-War**

8,403 were wounded

Appendix A

**Letter from Eisenhower
to Harris**

SUPREME HEADQUARTERS
ALLIED EXPEDITIONARY FORCE
Office of the Supreme Commander
13 July, 1944

Dear Harris:

Your recent performance in the Caen area was an eye opener to me, and emphasizes in my mind, again, the magnitude of the debt that this Allied Command owes to you and your officers and men. Your long record of pounding vital targets in Germany, of interrupting enemy communications, of preparing the way for our invasion forces and now, literally, becoming an agent in proper circumstances, of close battle support is one to excite praise and admiration.

I am truly proud to have you and your command in this Allied Team. We could not possibly get along without you.

Good luck!

Sincerely
DWIGHT EISENHOWER

Air Chief Marshal Sir Arthur T. Harris
KCB, OBE, AFC,
Air Officer Commanding-in-Chief,
Bomber Command

From: Page 319 The Royal Air Force and Two World Wars,
by Sir Maurice Dean, KCB, KCMG.

Appendix B

Extracts from the speech of Marshal of the Royal Air Force, Sir Arthur Harris, Bt, GCB, OBE, AFC, LLD. at the re-union dinner held at Grosvenor House Hotel, Park Lane, London, 30 April 1977.

In his opening remarks Sir Arthur said: 'As you know I am old, ga ga and garrulous . . . Whenever I speak of the Bomber Strategic offensive, I couple with it fifty-fifty our gallant American friends of the Eighth United States Air Force . . . You have never been given adequate recognition for what you did . . . you have been the object of articles of the type of authors, the types of journalist who knows perfectly well, that where he couldn't find a market for the ordinary tripe he's capable of, he can always sell a good sneerer or good smearer. But I get *my* facts straight from the horse's mouth; I don't go digging around at the other end of the animal, like those people I have referred to. And we have some very fine horses running for us, ranging from the most senior American Commanders, the most Senior British Commanders and, oddly enough, the most senior German Commanders of the last war'.

He then spoke of Albert Speer's background, saying: 'Albert Speer, when he came out of prison, wrote two books and he's been kind enough to send me copies of both those books and he's inscribed them and as well as the inscriptions . . . he said in his own words, of all the war books he's read, and he's read a lot of them, the effect of strategic bombing of Germany is *always* under estimated. And these are his own words, in his own handwriting and are repeated in the books, that the strategic bombing of Germany was the greatest lost battle for Germany of the whole of the war, greater than all the losses in all the retreats from Russia, in the surrender of their armies at Stalingrad . . .

'Starting right back in June '42, when we had barely started getting going, with about an eighth of the size of the force we required, and the Americans were just beginning to bring their Forces over here, there was a meeting among the higher ups in Germany, whether they would do this or that, and when it came to the question of whether they would develop the atom bomb, and don't forget, that before the war the Germans were ahead of everybody in that particular nefarious pursuit, when it came to that question, luckily for us and the world at large, Hitler dismissed it. He said, he'd have nothing to do with it because it was all Jews science . . .

'By the end of 1943, when we were getting a quarter of the force we had asked for, and the Americans had got going with their Mustang escort fighters, and we had already deprived the German armies at the Russian front by bomb damage to industry of 10,000 of their bigger calibre guns and 6,000 of their heaviest and medium heavy tanks, well that was quite a subscription towards the war, all done by the strategic bomber. But (Albert Speer) goes much further than that, that is he made that remark about the bomber strategic offensive being the greatest lost battle for Germany and goes on to explain why.

'The 8.8 centimetre dual purpose anti-aircraft and anti-tank gun was probably the most useful gun the Germans possessed and, as the armament, for instance, of their Tiger and Panther tanks, it was the only gun — mobile gun — capable of competing with the very heavy frontal armament of the Russian tanks. No less than 20,000 of those guns had to be taken away from the German armies on all their fronts, kept away from them and scattered all over Germany because of the unpredictability of where the strategic bombers were going to strike next. Speer said that reduced the anti-tank ability of the German Forces on all other of their fronts by half.

'Well, when you realise that no army on either side even advanced a yard without their armoured spearhead had busted a way through the defences, you can realise what it meant when the bombers, the strategic bombers, cut through their anti-tank defences by half.

'He went on to say that the requirement of being prepared to defend every German city and every German vital factory against the possibility — and the unpredicted probability — of bombing of any one of those particular places meant the stationing all over Germany of hundreds of thousands of men who should have been in the fighting forces.

'Field Marshal Erhard Milch, who commanded the German anti-aircraft defences, said he had nine hundred thousand fit men, he stressed the word fit men, in his anti-aircraft command alone. When he said fit, he meant fit to be used up in the front line of the German armies on the various fronts, not kicking their heels around Germany, waiting for the strategic bombers and wondering where they were going to strike next. Well, if you know of any individual army on the Allied side, which throughout the war, deprived the German armies of well over a million men, and half their anti-tank ability, I would personally be very obliged for the information . . . Around 2-300,000 men had to be retained, because as skilled tradesmen they had to be available, people such as plumbers, electricians, people who ran the synthetic oil manufacturing plants and railway workers . . . Now as I said, you don't seem to have got adequate credit for that anyhow in this country, but you'd certainly get it from the people who were immediately concerned, such as Eisenhower, Monty and the German Leaders . . .

'General Marshall referred to the fact that the joint Chiefs of Staff, in America had decided that our invasion of Europe was going so well, that the time had arrived to take away the direct command for the British and American bombers from Eisenhower, and return it to their respective commanders Sir

Charles Portal and General Arnold because those two heads of services had other theatres of war as well as Europe. Eisenhower replied — although Marshal expressed his apprehension that that would result in Eisenhower getting less support from Bomber Command than he'd been used to — Eisenhower said he had no such fear with regard to Bomber Command, one of the most effective parts of his entire organisation. Always seeking and finding and using new ways for their particular type of aircraft, to be of assistance in forwarding the progress of the armies on the ground . . . Now Monty was not given to praising lightly. I've heard him say on two occasions, both in vast banquets, he regards the British bombers as having been the greatest of all in the destruction of the German armies as a whole, and now that was pretty good coming from a soldier, not given to praising others lightly'.

Amid laughter Sir Arthur proceeded to make fun of articles by a man described as a well-known military correspondent who complained of two things, First: "All that Bomber Command ever did was to raise better obstacles in front of our armies than the Germans could have done themselves. In the other, we really took no part in the battle of Ardennes . . ." Regarding the first charge Sir Arthur pointed out that 'a bomb had not been invented that made a self-filling crater, for our troops to go forward . . . With regard to the second statement, Speer relates how upon Hitler's instructions he made his way, with the greatest difficulty to the Headquarters of the Armoured Division to see the German general and see how he meant to press on. General Sepp Deitrich replied, "Go on? How can I go on? We have no ammunition left and had all our supply lines cut by air attacks".

'The reason why it was you and nobody else (who cut their supply lines) is that in the atrocious weather that existed over those critical days and nights, all our bases, on the Continent

170

were almost permanently shut down and the American bases in East Anglia were shut down to an extent where they couldn't use their ordinary formations — escorted daylight tactics — but you fellows would get off in any muck and murk, even if they couldn't see, as one Cockney air-gunner remarked to me, "couldn't see yer 'and in front yer bloody fice" . . .

'They'd get off under those conditions provided there was somewhere to get down in the morning, and luckily where one base went out another came in, and so on . . . But you fellows did the job and Speer gives a very informative account of what he called, nocturnal discussion with Sepp Deitrich that night, as they sat there listening to the unrelenting roar of heavy four engined bombers overhead in the fog and the crash of bombs behind them, Sepp Deitrich remarked to him, "People don't understand that not even the best troops can stand the mass bombing, one experience of it and they lose all their fighting spirit". And Speer's concluding remark to that conversation was, "What a scene of German military impotence, we have no defence anywhere"'.

Harris pointed out, 'That remark of Sepp Deitrich, was not a patent to him by a long way. Shortly after our invasion got established in France, Rommel remarked to his superiors: "If you can't stop the bombing we cannot win, and it's no good going on, because all we get by going on is to lose another city every night. Make peace or drop the atom bomb if you've got it". He was not the only fellow to make that remark by a long way.

'As our Armies advanced along the coast of France, they urgently required the use of the Channel Ports such as Le Havre, Boulogne, Calais etc. Those ports were manned by 20,000 German soldiers . . . We were asked to bomb the massed defences, so we could get our fellows into those ports. They all surrendered, 20,000 troops for a total loss of 150 casualties to our army, thanks entirely to the massed bombing; and in the pocket diary of a senior German commander who surrendered at Boulogne were written these words, "Can anybody survive the carpet bombing? Sometimes one is driven to despair when at the mercy of the Royal Air Force without protection. It seems like all fighting and all losses are in vain."

'Well there you are, one after another, the German Generals said the same thing. Now when it came to our side and the American side I told you what Eisenhower thought of us; but after the bombing which did so much at the Battle of the Ardennes, he sent me a thank you message, and I replied thanking him for his message, and I said that message had been passed to the crews responsible, and I finished my signal by saying, "You know you can always depend on my lads for anything short of the impossible". Tedder relates how that signal of mine, circulated around Eisenhower's HQ, and scrawled across my signal in Eisenhower's own hand-writing were the words "Godammit they've already achieved the impossible . . ."

'Now there's a famous military — a so-called famous military — correspondent saying that, "Bomber Command did nothing but make an infernal nuisance of themselves," where our Armies were concerned on the Continent, and the Commander in Chief saying, "You fellows achieved the impossible on behalf of the Armies." Who do you like to believe?

'Quite apart from the facts that I've given you . . .(which are emphasised) beyond doubt with Albert Speer's statement that the strategic bomber was the greatest of all their losses in the war, I would say you also scored the biggest air victory of the war, because you did what "Boom" (Trenchard) said was the one thing you had to do to defeat the enemy, drive him on the defensive, and you certainly did that over the last year or two of the war, the Germans did nothing with their air force, which had been the major cause of their early sweep across Europe, Poland and everywhere else at the beginning of the war and their early victories. But they did nothing over the last year or two but made fighters and twin fighter bombers, in a despairing effort, which failed in its object to protect the Fatherland from the strategic bombers, and that was a fact.

'The effect was that firstly it put an entire stop to the bombing of this country. Its quite true they started off with their comic rockets and things, well you know, the V2 rocket for instance, the thing that created quite a lot of alarm and despondency. The maximum production of those V2 rockets a thousand a month, and it took 5,000 of them to carry as much explosive as one attack of the Strategic American and British bombers, so there's a comparative value.

'Now I've told you I think you won certainly one of the major land battles (and through) what I've told you about Albert Speer, certainly one of the major air battles in driving them entirely on the defensive. But what you've never been given any credit for — you only won the major sea battle of the European war.

'Who said that? Albert Speer again.

'I have read an account of the so-called expert naval correspondent who said, "In the whole of the war Bomber Command only sank one submarine." What did Albert Speer say? (And) he was responsible for the production of submarines and everything else. This single sentence in one of his books, "We would have kept to our promised output of submarines for Admiral Dönitz's U-boat fleet if the bombers had not sunk a third of them in the ports".

'Who was right? The Navy who wanted to pinch all our Lancasters to go looking for haystacks all over the Atlantic, looking for needles in the haystacks, or we, who said, send the planes to get the submarines where they came from, not where they went to. But that was only the beginning of the naval war. The German Admiral in charge of the training of U-boat crews wrote a letter in which he said, "Without trained U-boat crews you cannot have a U-boat offensive, and I can't train crews if you can't keep the damned air-laid mines away from my training ground."

'Well, they couldn't keep them away, although the major expensive effort of the German navy during the war was trying to counter the 30,000 tons of mines that you fellows laid in waters approaching every port that the Germans used from the Baltic, through the whole of the North Sea coast, down to the Bay of Biscay, and you can be quite certain from the wreckage they caused, those mines certainly accounted for quite a number of other submarines who disappeared - sunk without trace.

'And those mines coupled with the bombing virtually annihilated the German merchant marine, on which they depended for the import of vital ores from Scandinavia for their basic industries . . . (At) the beginning of the war the Germans had a High Seas Fleet, consisting of some 17 absolutely super battle wagons, ranging all the way from the big fellows, the *Tirpitz* and *Bismarck* — Willie Tait finished the *Tirpitz* with his merry boys . . . What happened to the rest of them, do you ever hear? The Navy sank one. The Fleet Air Arm sank one. The Norwegians sank one; the Russians Navy did so much damage to one it was out of action for the whole of the war. Bomber Command kept two out of action by repeated damage and sank *six*, and really haven't got a thank you for it.

'The two left in the closing stages of the war, *Prinz Eugen* and the *Nuremberg*, were laying just outside of Copenhagen, cold meat to the bombs that Willie Tait and Co., were just putting on their machines: I happened to be out of the office for five minutes — occasionally I had to leave my office for five minutes — my Deputy Commander had taken a half day off — one of six half days he took off during the entire war — either to attend to his own business, or had his business attended to him — and my naval liaison officer, who was an absolutely first class fellow and of the utmost assistance to us

174

with the mining, when I got back to my office, there he was all a tremble and he said, "I had to countermand the attack on the *Eugen* and the *Nuremberg*", I said, "Countermand, why?" He said, "Orders from the Admiralty".

'Well, of course you couldn't blame the lad, I mean, to a Naval Officer an order from the Admiralty is one above a direct command from the Almighty. So he'd done it — and by that time it was too late to turn the bombers back again . . . The fact (the German battleships) were allowed to escape, allowed them to rather spitefully . . . expend most of their ammunition in and around Copenhagen, doing a lot of damage and killing a lot of our Danish friends and would-be Allies.

'Well, take into account what we did to the submarines and don't forget, (but) I forgot to tell you that when the destruction in the ports became absolutely intolerable, the Germans had a bright idea. They would pre-fabricate their submarines inland, send the huge sections down to the ports, so they would only be a few days or weeks being buttoned together, rather than being many months being built from the keel upwards and destroyed in the process by bombers. But that didn't work either. Because the pre-fabricated sections were too big to go by rail or road. They could only go by canal. Which was exactly why the strategic bomber, American and British, kept on busting up the two canals concerned, the Mittelland canal and the Dortmund Ems. With the result that the delivery of those prefabricated sections to the ports quickly sank from a maximum of 120 sections in a month to a few handfuls and then to zero.

'Well I hope I've told you enough about your share in the air war, in the naval war and in the land war, and nobody can take that away from you, because I say it's all from the horse's mouth, from the leading German, leading American and the leading British — even Lord Alanbrooke, the head of the Army, who was no friend of the Air Force — always making inordinate demands of what we should do for them, he admitted in his private diaries, which were published after the war by Sir Arthur Bryant, he referred to the brilliant skills of the bombers and the outstanding assistance to the Army during the invasion'.

Marshal of the Royal Air Force, Sir Arthur Harris, Bt, GCB, OBE, AFC, LLD concluded 'Well, when you consider that our invasion of France consisted of 37 divisions with a large content of green and inexperienced troops, and that in our experience in the First World War, soldiers always said, if you want any chance of success in the attack, you must have two to one advantage in numbers and materiel over the enemy. Those 37 divisions chased 60 German divisions clear across Europe, from the Atlantic to the Elbe and totally destroyed the German Army of half a million men.

'The 7th Army captured tens of thousands of prisoners, all their equipment and beat them down to an unconditional surrender at Lüneberg Heath, and that was largely due to two things; the Germans lack of anti-tank defences and the complete, not air superiority, but absolute air supremacy of our fellows over the Continent.

'Thanks to the fact that the bombers had forced the German Air Force to expend nearly all its efforts on a failed attempt to defend their own country.

'Thank you for listening to me'. *

* Extracts taken from Ray Callow's recording entitled, "The Way it Was". The tape can be obtained from the Bomber Command Association, Royal Air Force Museum, Hendon.

Appendix C

SPECIAL ORDER OF THE DAY FROM AIR CHIEF MARSHAL SIR A. T. HARRIS, KCB, OBE, AFC

12th May 1945

Men and women of Bomber Command —

More than five and a half years ago, within hours of a declaration of war, Bomber Command first assailed the German enemy.

You were then but a handful, inadequate in everything but the skill and determination of the crews for that sombre occasion and for the unknown years of unceasing battle which lay beyond horizons black indeed.

You, the aircrew of Bomber Command, sent your first ton of bombs away on the morrow of the outbreak of war. A million tons of bombs and mines have followed from Bomber Command alone; from Declaration of War to Cease Fire a continuity of battle without precedent and without relent.

In the battle of France your every endeavour bore down upon an overwhelming and triumphant enemy.

After Dunkirk your country stood alone — in arms but largely unarmed — between the Nazi tyranny and domination of the world.

The Battle of Britain in which you took a great part, raised the last barrier, strained but holding, in the path of the all conquering Wehrmacht, and the bomb smoke of the Channel ports choked back down German throats the very word "Invasion": not again to find the expression within these narrow seas until the bomb-disrupted defences of the Normandy beach-heads fell to our combined assault.

In the long years between much was to pass.

Then it was that you, and you for long alone, carried the war ever deeper and even more furiously into the heart of the Third Reich. There the whole might of the German enemy in undivided strength and — scarcely less a foe — the very elements, arrayed against you. You overcame them both.

Through those desperate years, undismayed by any odds, undeterred by any casualties, night succeeding night, you fought: the Phalanx of the United Nations.

You fought alone, as the one force then assailing German soil, you fought alone as individuals — isolated in your crew stations by the darkness and the murk, and from all other aircraft in company.

Not for you the hot emulation of high endeavour in the glare and panoply of martial array. Each crew, each one in each crew, fought alone through black nights rent only, mile after continuing mile, by the fiercest barrages ever raised and the instant sally of the searchlights. In each dark minute of those long miles lurked menace. Fog, ice, snow and tempest found you undeterred.

In that loneliness in action lay the final test, the ultimate stretch of human staunchness and determination.

Your losses mounted through those years, years in which your chance of survival through one spell of operational duty was negligible; through two periods, mathematically Nil. Nevertheless survivors pressed forward as volunteers to pit their desperately acquired skill in even a third period of operations, on special tasks.

In those five years and eight months of continuous battle over enemy soil, your casualties over long periods were grievous. As the count is cleared, those of Bomber Command who gave their lives to bring near to impotence an enemy who had surged swift in triumph through the a Continent, and to enable the United Nations to deploy in full array, will be found not less than the total dead of our National Invasion Armies now in Germany. In the whole history of our National Forces, never have so small a band of men been called to support so long such odds. You indeed bore the brunt.

With it all you never ceased to rot the very heart out of the enemy's war resources and resistance.

His Capital and near 100 of his cities and towns, including nearly all of leading war industrial importance, lie in utter ruin together with the greater part of the war industry which they supported.

Thus you brought to nought the enemy's original advantage of an industrial might intrinsically greater than ours and supported by the labour of captive millions, now set free.

For the first time in more than a century you have brought home to the habitual aggressor of Europe the full and acrid flavours of war, so long the perquisite of his victims.

All this and much more, have you achieved during the five and a half years of continuous battle, despite all opposition from an enemy disposing of many a geographical and strategical advantage with which to exploit an initial superiority in numbers.

Men from every part of the Empire and most of the Allied Nations fought in our ranks. Indeed a band of brothers.

In the third year of the war the Eighth Bomber Command, and the Fifteenth Bomber Command, USAAF from their Mediterranean bases, ranged themselves at our side, zealous in extending every mutual aid, vieing in every assault upon our common foe. Especially they played the leading part in sweeping the enemy fighter defences from our path, and finally, out of the skies.

Nevertheless, nothing that the crews accomplished - and it was much, and decisive — could have been achieved without the devoted service of every man and woman in the Command.

Those who attended the aircraft, mostly in the open, through six bitter winters: endless intricacies in a prolonged misery of wet and cold. They rightly earned the implicit trust of the crews. They set extraordinary records of aircraft serviceability. Those who manned the Stations, Operational Headquarters, Supply lines and Communications.

To you who survive I would say this. Content yourselves, and take credit for those who perished, that now the "Cease Fire" has sounded, countless homes within our Empire will welcome back a father, a husband, or a son, whose life, but for your endeavours and your sacrifices, would assuredly have been expended during long years of agony, to achieve a victory already ours. No Allied Nation is clear of this debt to you.

I cannot here expound your full achievements.

Your attack on the industrial centres of Northern Italy did much towards the collapse of the Italian and German Armies in North Africa, and to further the invasion of the Italian mainland.

Of the German enemy, two to three million fit men, potentially vast armies, were continuously held throughout the War in direct and indirect defence against your assaults. A great part of her industrial war effort went towards fending your attacks.

You struck a critical proportion of the weapons of war from enemy hands, on every front. You immobilised armies, leaving them shorn of supplies, reinforcements, resources and reserves, the easier prey to our advancing forces

You eased and abetted the passage of our troops over major obstacles. You blasted the enemy from long prepared defences where he essayed to hold: on the Normandy beaches, at the hinge of the battle for Caen, in the jaws of the Falaise Gap, to the strong-points of the enemy-held Channel Ports, St Vith, Houffalize, and the passage of the Rhine. In battle after battle you sped our armies to success at minimum cost to our troops. The Commanders of our land forces, and indeed those of the enemy, have called your attacks decisive.

You enormously disrupted every enemy means of communication, the very life-blood of his military and economic machines. Railways, canals, and every form of transport fell first to decay and then to chaos under your assaults. You so shattered the enemy's oil plants as to deprive him of all but the final trickle of fuel. His aircraft became earthbound, his road transport ceased to roll. Armoured fighting vehicles lay helpless outside of battle, or fell immobilised into our hands. His strategic and tactical plans failed through inability to move.

From his war industries supplies of ore, coal, steel, fine metals, aircraft, guns, ammunition, tanks, vehicles and every ancillary equipment, dwindled under your attack.

At the very crisis of the invasion of Normandy, you virtually annihilated the German naval surface forces then in the Channel; a hundred craft and more fell victim to those three attacks.

You sank or damaged a large but yet untotalled number of enemy submarines in his ports and by mine-laying in his waters. You interfered widely and repeatedly with his submarine training programmes.

With extraordinary accuracy, regardless of opposition, you hit and burst through every carapace which he could devise to protect his submarines in harbour. By your attacks on inland industries and coastal ship-yards you caused hundreds of his submarines to be stillborn.

Your mine-laying throughout the enemy's sea lanes, your bombing of his inland waters, and his ports, confounded his sea traffic and burst his canals. From Norway throughout the Baltic, from Jutland to the Gironde, on the coasts of Italy and North Africa, you laid and re-laid the minefields. The wreckage of the enemy's naval and merchant fleets litter and encumbers his sea-lanes and dockyards. A thousand known ships, and many more as yet unknown, fell casualty to your mines.

You hunted and harried his major warships from hide to hide. You put out of action, gutted or sank most of them.

By your attacks on Experimental Stations, factories, communications and firing sites, you long postponed and much reduced the V weapon attacks. You averted an enormous further toll of death and destruction from your Country.

The pilots of the Photographic Reconnaissance Units, without whose lonely ventures far and wide over enemy territory we should have been largely powerless to plan or to strike.

The Operational Crew Training Organisation of the Command, which through the years of ceaseless work by day and night never failed, in the face of every difficulty and unpredicted call, to replace all casualties and to keep our constantly expanding first line up to strength in crews trained to the highest pitch of efficiency; simultaneously producing nearly 20,000 additional trained aircrew for the raising and reinforcement of some 50 extra squadrons, formed in the Command and despatched for service in other Commands at home and overseas.

The men and women of the Meteorological Branch who attained prodigious exactitudes in a fickle art and stood brave on assertion where science is inexact. Time and again they saved us from worse than the enemy could have achieved. Their record is outstanding.

The meteorological reconnaissance pilots, who flew through anything and everything in search of the feasible.

The operational Research Sections whose meticulous

investigation of every detail of every attack provided data for the continuous confounding of the enemy and the consistent reduction of our own casualties.

The scientists, especially those of the Telecommunications Research Establishment, who placed in unending succession in our hands the technical means to resolve our problems and to confuse the every parry of the enemy. Without their skill and labours beyond doubt we could not have prevailed.

The Works Services who engineered, for Bomber Command alone, 2,000 miles of runway track and road, with all that goes with them.

The Works Staff, Designers, and Workers who equipped and re-equipped us for Battle. Their efforts; their honest workmanship, kept in our hand indeed a Shining Sword.

To all of you I would say how proud I am to have served in Bomber Command for four and a half years, and to have been your Commander-in-Chief through more than three years of your saga.

Your task in the German war is now completed. Famously have you fought. Well have you deserved of your Country and her Allies.

(sgd) A. T. Harris
Air Chief Marshal
Commanding-in-Chief
Bomber Command

(Page 25, *The Marker* - Winter 1990)

Bibliography

Andrews, Allen: *The Air Marshals*, Macdonald 1970

Ashworth, Chris: *R.A.F. Bomber Command,* Patrick Stephens 1995

Bauer, Lt.Col: *History of World War II*, Gallery Press

Boog, Horst: *Sir Arthur Harris, Dispatch on War Operations*
    Frank Cass 1995

Bowyer, Chaz: *Tales from the Bombers*, William Kimber 1985

Brown, David *with* Christopher Shores & Kenneth Mackey,
    Guinness History of Air Warfare 1976
    Guinness Superlatives

Carrington, Charles: *Soldier at Bomber Command*, Leo Cooper 1987

Cheshire, G/Cpt: *Bomber Pilot*, White Lion 1973

Clutton-Brock, Oliver: *Massacre Over the Marne*,
    Patrick Stephens 1984

Cox, Sebastian: *Sir Arthur Harris, Dispatch on War Operations*
    Frank Cass 1995

Cox, Sebastian: *The Strategic Air War Against Germany 1939-1945*
    Frank Cass 1998

Dean, Sir Maurice: *The R.A.F. in Two World Wars,* Cassell 1979

Delve, Ken *with* Peter Jacobs: *The Six-Year Offensive,*
    Arms & Armour Press 1992

Fyfe, James: *The Great Ingratitude*, G.C. Book Publishers, 1993

Goulding, A.G: *Uncommon Valour*, Merlin Books 1985

Hampton, James: *Selected For Aircrew*, Air Research
    Publications 1993

Harris, Sir Arthur: *Bomber Offensive,* Collins 1947

Harris, MRAF Sir Arthur: *The Way It Was*, Ray Callow

Hastings, Max: *Bomber Command,* Michael Joseph 1979

Hughes, Jimmy: *Special Order of the Day*, The Marker, Winter 1990

Jablenski, Edward: *Flying Fortress*, Sidgwick & Jackson 1974

Jackson, Robert: *Before the Storm*, Arthur Baker Ltd 1972

Kaplan, Philip *with* Jack Currie: *Round The Clock*, Cassell 1994

Keegan, John: *History of Warfare,* Hutchinson 1993

Lewis, Bruce: *Aircrew*, Leo Cooper 1991

Longmate, Norman: *The Bombers*, Hutchinson 1983

Maitland, Andrew: *Through the Bombsight*, William Kimber 1986

Messenger, Charles: *Bomber Harris*, Arms & Armour 1984

Middlebrook, Martin *with* Chris Everitt: *The Bomber Command War Diaries*, Viking 1987

Mitchen, Samuel W *with* Gene Mueller: *Hitler's Commanders* Cooper 1992

Morrison, Wilbur H: *Fortress Without a Roof,* S. Martins Press 1986

Musgrove, Gordon: *Pathfinder Force*, Macdonald & James Publishing 1976

Overy, R.J: *The Air War 1939–1945*, Papermac 1980

Overy, R.J: *Why the Allies Won the War,* Jonathan Cape 1988

Regan, Geoffrey: *The Guinness Book of Military Blunders* Guinness Publications 1991

Richards, Denis: *The Hardest Victory*, Hodder & Stoughton 1994

Richards, Denis: *Portal of Hungerford*, Heinemann 1997

Richards, Denis: *R.A.F. 1939–45 Vol.1,* H.M.Stationery Office 1954

Richards, Denis & Hilary St.G: *R.A.F.1939–45 Vol.11,* H.M.Stationery Office 1954

Saunders,Hilary St.G: *R.A.F. 1939–45 Vol.111,* H.M.Stationery Office 1954

Saward, G/Capt Dudley: *Bomber Harris*, Cassell Ltd & Enright Publishers 1984

Searby, A/Cdr. John: *The Bomber Battle for Berlin*, Airlife Publications 1991

Searby, A/Cdr. John: *Everlasting Arms,* William Kimber 1988

Spaight, J. M: *Bombing Vindicated*, Geoffrey Bles 1944

Speer, Albert: *Inside the Third Reich*, Weidenfeld & Nicholson 1970

Taylor, A.J.P: *English History 1914–45*, Clarendon Press 1965

Tedder, Lord: *Air Power in War*, Hodder & Stoughton

Terraine, John: *A Time of Courage*, Macmillan Publishing 1985

Terraine, John: *Right of the Line*, Hodder & Stoughton 1985

Webster, Sir Charles *with* Noble Frankland: *Strategic Air Offensive*
        Against Germany Vols. I, II, III, IV,
        H. M. Stationery Office 1961
Report of the British Bombing Survey Unit: *The Strategic Air War*
        Against Germany, 1939–1943, Frank Cass 1998

Further Reading

R L Austen: *High Adventure, A Navigator at War*
Air Vice Marshal D.C.T. Bennett: *Pathfinder*
Chaz Bowyer: *History of the RAF*
Chaz Bowyer: *Pathfinders at War*
Chaz Bowyer: *Guns in the Sky*
Chaz Bowyer: *Bomber Barons*
Andrew Brookes: *Bomber Squadrons at War*
James Campbell: *The Bombing of Nuremberg*
Chas Chandler: *Tail Gunner*
Don Charlwood: *No Moon Tonight*
Alan W. Cooper: *The Men who Breached the Dams*
Alan W. Cooper: *Air Battles over the Ruhr*
Jack Currie: *Lancaster Target*
Mike Garbett & Brian Goulding: *Lancaster at War*
Mike Garbett & Brian Goulding: *Lancaster at War 2*
G. Gray: *Green Markers Ahead Skipper*
Bill Gunsten (editor): *So Many, a folio dedicated to all those*
        who served with the RAF 1939–45
John B. Hilling: *Strike Hard*
Geoffrey Jones: *Night Flight*
G/Cpt. T. G. Mahaddie DSO, DFC, AFC, CZMG, CENG, FRAes:
        Hamish, The Memoirs of
John Maynard: *Bennett & the Pathfinders*

Martin Middlebrook: *The Peenemünde Raid*
Martin Middlebrook: *The Nuremberg Raid*
Martin Middlebrook: *The Battle of Hamburg*
Gordon Musgrove: *Operation Gomorrah*
Richard Overy: *Bomber Command 1939–45*
Richard Passmore: *Blenheim Boys*
G/Cpt. Tom Sawyer DFC: *Only Owls & Bloody Fools Fly at Night*
Ron Smith DFM: *Rear Gunner Pathfinders*
Tony Spooner: *Clean Sweep*
Walter Thompson DFC & Bar: *Lancaster to Berlin*
Alex Thorne DSO, DFC: *Lancaster at War 4 Pathfinder Squadron*
Anthony Verrier: *The Bomber Offensive*
G. F. Wallace: *Guns of the RAF*
Dr. Roland Winfield DFC, AFC: *The Sky Belongs to Them*

Acknowledgements

Grateful acknowledgment is made for the use of copyright material as follows: -

- James Fyffe. *The Great Ingratitude.*
- Chris Ashworth. *RAF Bomber Command.*
- Philip Kaplan and Jack Currie. *Round the Clock.*
- James Hampton. *Selected for Aircrew.*
- Mrs Diana Searby. A/Cdr John Searby's *Everlasting Arms & Bomber Battle for Berlin.*
- Mrs Peggy Goulding. A.G. Goulding's *Uncommon Valour.*
- Chaz Bowyer. *Tales from the Bombers.*
- John Thomas literary executor. Charles Carrington's *Soldier at Bomber Command.*
- Bruce Lewis. *Aircrew.*
- Charles Messenger. *Bomber Harris.*
- The Hon. Mrs Jackie Assheton, daughter of MRAF Sir Arthur Harris. *Bomber Offensive.*
- Denis Richards. *The Hardest Victory & Portal of Hungerford.*
- Norman Longmate. *The Bombers.*
- Crown Copyright material is produced with the permission of the Controller of Her Majesty's Stationery Office. *The Strategic Air Offensive Against Germany 1939/1945* by Sir C Webster and N Frankland & *The Royal Air Force 1939-1945* by Denis Richard & Hilary St G Saunders.
- Martin Middlebrook & Chris Everitt. *The Bomber Command Diaries.*
- Oliver Clutton-Brock. *Massacre Over The Marne.*
- Little Brown & Co. Allen Andrews, *The Air Marshals* & Gordon Musgrove, *Pathfinder Force.*
- Ray Callow. *Recording The Way It Was.*
- Geoffrey Regan. *The Guinness Book of Military Blunders.*
- Jimmy Hughes DFM. *Special Order of the Day from Air Chief Marshal A. T. Harris KCB, OBE, AFC* from *The Marker*, Winter 1990.
- Mrs Janet Saward wife of G/Cap. Dudley Saward. *Bomber Harris.*
- Ken Delve and Peter Jacobs. *The Six Year Offensive.*
- Crown Copyright. Photographs from the Photographic Archive Imperial War Museum.

- Robert Jackson. *Before the Storm.*
- Max Hastings. *Bomber Command.*
- *The Guardian*
- *The Observer*
- *Daily Express*
- *Daily Mail*
- *The Daily Telegraph*
- *The Sunday Times*
- *The Times*
- *T.V. Times*
- *The Sunday Telegraph*
- *The Spectator.*
- *Independent on Sunday*

I am also indebted to:-
- Lt.Col Bauer. *History of World War II.*
- Host Boog in Sir Arthur Harris' *Dispatch on War Operations.*
- Sir Maurice Dean. *The RAF in Two World Wars.*
- G/Capt. L Cheshire. *Bomber Pilot.*
- David Brown, Christopher Shores, Kenneth Mackay. *Guinness History of Air Warfare.*
- Edward Jablenski. *Flying Fortress.*
- Samuel W. Mitchan and Gene Mueller. *Hitler's Commanders.*
- Wilber H. Morrison. *Fortress Without a Roof.*
- R. J. Overy. *The Air War 1939-1945* & *Why the Allies Won the War.*
- J.M. Spaight. *Bombing Vindicated.*
- Albert Speer. *Inside the Third Reich.*
- A.J.P. Taylor. *English History 1914-1945.*
- Lord Tedder. *Air Power in War.*
- John Terraine. *The Right of the Line* & *A Time of Courage.*
- Sebastian Cox. Editorial: Sir Arthur T. Harris *Dispatch on War Operations. The Strategic Air War Against Germany 1939-1945.*
- Francois Prins. Tribute to Sir Arthur Harris in *Flypast* June 84.
- Toronto Star. *Death By Moonlight.*
- BBC, ITV and CHANNEL 4

Especially, I should like to record my thanks for the encouragement and support given by the late Brian Wickins and the patience of my wife and family, particularly my daughter Pip who helped to type and edit the manuscript; to Ken Pickering, Heather and Mike Berry who helped to proof read and for the front cover from a painting by Heather Berry; to Dr Bob Kapur for amending the disk; to the staff of the Rotherham Central Library for their unstinting assistance; to Doug Radcliffe MBE, Secretary, Bomber Command Association and Philip Howard for advice and assistance.

Finally, I offer my thanks to Air Marshal Sir Ivor Broom KCB. CBE. DSO. DFC**. AFC. for kindly contributing a Foreword to this book. For the good wishes expressed by so many of the authors from whose books I have quoted I will always be grateful.

Every effort has been made to obtain the author's permission for the use of any quoted material, but if any breach has occurred it has been entirely unintentional and without malice.

About the Author

Born in July 1924, Kenneth Harder volunteered for service in the RAF and was accepted for Aircrew in March 1942. After Initial and Elementary Training he was selected to be a Navigator on Mosquitos, but when he discovered this would involve another two years of training he asked to transfer to an Air Gunnery course and from thence through OTU went through the Heavy Conversion Unit and the Pathfinder School to 635 Squadron at Downham Market, where he flew Lancasters as a Mid-Upper Gunner.

After two consecutive tours — fifty-six operations — a commission, DFC and the Permanent Award of the Pathfinder Force wings, he was posted to join a crew testing the Lincoln bomber destined for *Tiger Force* — to hit Japan in August 1945. Happily, Japan surrendered before this force was used and the author joined the ranks of unemployed aircrew, from whence he remustered to Transport Command as a Traffic Officer. The postings which followed took him all over the Far East and Australasia, which stood him in very good stead for a future civilian career as a respected Travel Consultant in London. Subsequently moving and settling in Rotherham South Yorkshire where he became Managing Director of a small chain of travel agents.

As members of an ever-dwindling band of people who actually *served* in the Second World War, both the author and his publisher feel it is important that the story of the war waged by Bomber Command which contributed so much to eventual victory, should be properly and accurately told.

This book achieves that aim and so offers to post-war generations a true account of how the lives of those thousands of very young men who sacrificed themselves taking the war to the enemy, when no-one else could, made that ultimate victory possible.